The Book of Melba

The annual Kresge Eminent Artist Award salutes an exceptional artist in the visual, performing, or literary arts for lifelong professional achievements to metropolitan Detroit's cultural community

Melba Joyce Boyd is the 2023 Kresge Eminent Artist. This monograph salutes her life and her art making.

Melba Joyce Boyd in Detroit, MI, in 1970. Photo: Leni Sinclair, 2016 Kresge Eminent Artist, Getty Images.

The Book of Melba

Melba Joyce Boyd
2023 Kresge Eminent Artist

Nichole Christian
Creative Director, Editor and Lead Writer

Edward Ryan (E-A-R)
Graphic Design and Art Direction

with contributions from
Erin Kirkland, Zak Rosen and Maya Wynn Boyd

THE KRESGE FOUNDATION

Table of Contents

Intro

10	**Foreword** Rip Rapson
12	**Artist's Statement** Melba Joyce Boyd
14	**Welcome to The Book of Melba: A Multiverse** Nichole M. Christian

Respect

28	**Literary peers, family, and friends discuss Melba Joyce Boyd's creative and cultural legacy.** Nichole M. Christian

Roots

46	**Melba reflects on her parents' defining choice to leave behind multigenerational roots in Alabama for the promise of prosperity in Detroit.**

Rise

60	**Melba recounts discovering her voice, a trailblazing mentor and unexpected place amid the Black Arts Movement and Detroit's simultaneous racial justice protests.**

Outro

78	**Melba's Garden: Poems and Excerpted Essays**
104	**Select Works, Citations, and Awards**
112	**Kresge Arts in Detroit**
113	**2023 Kresge Advisory Panel**
113	**The Eminent Artist Award**
114	**Past Eminent Artists**
116	**Credits and Acknowledgements**
118	**Index**

Intro

Foreword

Rip Rapson

President and CEO, The Kresge Foundation

Consider for a moment the honor roll of Kresge Eminent Artists since the first in 2008: Charles McGee, Marcus Belgrave, Bill Harris, Naomi Long Madgett, David DiChiera…Bill Rauhauser, Ruth Adler Schnee, Leni Sinclair, Patricia Terry-Ross… Wendell Harrison, Gloria House, Marie Woo, Shirley Woodson and Olayami Dabls.

Painters and poets, a playwright, an impresario, two photographers, three consummate musicians, a ceramicist and a textile artist, cultural activists, placemakers and educators… most of whom check more than a single box in their careers. They all have made outsized contributions to our community and made their vision felt beyond the community of metropolitan Detroit. They have been hometown heroes and ambassadors for their city and their art forms.

To this esteemed group, we are proud to add Dr. Melba Joyce Boyd. She is yet another of these fulcrums of creativity. She is a scholar of her forerunners in the African American literary tradition, and an artist who very much draws inspirations from those forerunners. She stands on the shoulders of giants and is now a giant in her own right on whose shoulders she invites others to stand. Her story, she tells us, is "absolutely a Detroit story." And as she has written about her Detroit contemporaries, she herself has been "nurtured in the vitality and complexity of a city bound to the grit and bravado of urban struggle."

In these pages, we strive to tell her story — often bringing to the fore her own words on the page and in audio recordings. And we share her artistry, highlighting often-out-of-print poems and hard-to-find essays.

We do this in the spirit that has guided our Eminent Artist monographs since the beginning. We seek to elevate artists and artistry in our community, to reaffirm our belief in the ability of arts and culture to root us in the past (painful as it might be), to give cohesiveness to our lives today … to inspire our own creativity, to hopefully see anew the possibilities for tomorrow.

Artist's Statement

Melba Joyce Boyd
2023

I'm doing what you're supposed to do as an artist; I didn't come up with it. Since the beginning of time, poets, writers, even songwriters, have been documenting what has happened, trying to connect it to something that carries deeper meaning than necessarily the moments or incidents. You're trying to help people reconcile. It's an ongoing story. I'm just a part of it.

i write as a reason to be
i write poetry that bleeds
i write to stop the pain

From *yari yari: writing for the future*

Welcome to The Book of Melba: A Multiverse

Nichole M. Christian

Dr. Melba Joyce Boyd. Dr. Boyd. Oma. Melba. She goes by many names and navigates multiple labels. Each human life defies easy summation, some more so than others. Melba Joyce Boyd is one of those.

Her layered journey as a poet, essayist, biographer, editor, professor and filmmaker epitomizes the notion of multi-dimensionality. Melba's life and creative achievements deserve full immersion and in ways that simultaneously celebrate her contributions and offer an overdue primer for those yet to know the name and the legacy it represents. May the facts of Melba's life – as she's dared to live and to share them – illuminate her story anew.

FACT 1:
Melba Joyce Boyd believes in the power of poetry.

She has devoted more than five decades of her life amplifying poetry as an art form and mentoring new voices in Detroit, the place of her birth, April 2, 1950.

FACT 2:
The "M" in Melba is an emblem of one of her greatest truths: She is many things at once, by choice.

She is, somewhat famously, a wearer of many hats – stylish and bold. The hats tell you that Melba is present. She is someone to know.

Of course, it's Melba Joyce Boyd's multiplicity that makes her name most memorable. She is: Melba the award-winning poet, Melba the distinguished professor, Melba the essayist, Melba the biographer, Melba the editor, Melba the documentary filmmaker, the historian, the community connector, the mentor, the sister, the mother, the cherished Oma (grandmother to Kyler, 18, John IV, 13, Lukas, 6, Zoe, 4, and Maverick, 6).

"Melba-the-marvel" is how her longtime publisher Dennis Teichman sums up the poet and the woman. Four of Melba's nine poetry books were published by Teichman's Past Tents Press. "She's sort of the epitome of what Whitman means when he says, 'I contain multitudes.'[1] She has an amazing track record even now of putting out work, not just poetry, everywhere, and it's usually work that, over time, still means something."

Melba's husband, James Kenyon, says her many facets are fused by a single fact. "Melba has a big brain," he explains, "but she has an even bigger heart for people. That's what she loves. She understands that the human race is not perfect, that there's violence, police brutality, discrimination all around the world, and it bothers her deeply. It's why she doesn't really write about herself so much. She wants you to see the people, not her."

Kenyon, a retired corporate communications writer, is often awestruck by how much Melba remains in motion. Her career spans more than five decades and stretches across five different disciplines. This is why many call her "a force."

Prolific since her college days at Western Michigan University, Melba has published 13 books, including her nine poetry collections. She has written biographies and created films about Black literary giants including 2012 Kresge Eminent Artist Naomi Long Madgett and Dudley Randall, founder of Broadside Press, the pioneering Detroit-based Black-owned publishing imprint. Melba has authored two award-winning surveys of Randall's legacy: *Roses and Revolutions: The Selected Writings of Dudley Randall* (2009), and his official biography, *Wrestling with the Muse: Dudley Randall and the Broadside Press* (2003).

Prior to his death in 2000, Randall surprised Melba, his former protégée and assistant editor, by naming her in his will as his official biographer. Broadside was the literary home of notable African American poets including Gwendolyn Brooks, Nikki Giovanni, Etheridge Knight, Audre Lorde, Haki Madhubuti, Naomi Long Madgett, the 2012 Kresge Eminent Artist, and Dr. Gloria House, the 2019 Kresge Eminent Artist.

"Probably one of the reasons that Dudley picked her," says Gregory J. Reed, a friend, longtime prominent Detroit attorney and the founding chairman of the city's Entertainment Commission, "is that he knew she would be a person that would be on guard for his legacy."

Reed met Melba when she was in the fourth grade. "She was raised to be a person of intellect and impact. I've always admired that about her, that she's fearless and mouthy but in a way that moves your thinking," Reed explains as he laughs. "With Melba, it's always been, 'What in the hell is she saying now?'"

Melba has written more than 100 essays about poets, the Black Arts and Civil Rights movements, Detroit, and various cultural legends for an array of anthologies, academic journals, and newspapers in the United States and Europe. German and French translators have brought out her works in translation with more on the way.

Cover art from *blues music sky of mourning: the German poems*, published in 2006.

Her resume overflows with local, state and national honors including multiple Library of Michigan Notable Book awards and a 2010 Independent Publishers Award; in 2010, she was a finalist for the NAACP Image Award for Poetry. *Roses and Revolutions: The Selected Writings of Dudley Randall* (2009), won the 2010 Independent Publishers Award, the 2010 Library of Michigan Notable Book award, and was a finalist for the NAACP Image Award and the Foreword Book Award for Poetry. *Wrestling with the Muse: Dudley Randall and the Broadside Press* received a 2004 Honor Award from the Black Caucus of the American Library Association.

TOP Melba with students, colleagues and husband James Kenyon at Fudan University in Shanghai, China, in 2009.
LEFT Melba Joyce Boyd and John Percy Boyd III, her eldest child.
RIGHT Melba with her daughter Maya and son John Percy Boyd III.

Melba the scholar shines too. She was a visiting professor at Fudan University in Shanghai, China, in 2009. Melba was also a Fulbright scholar at the University of Bremen in what was then West Germany, an experience she describes as formative to her work as a scholar and as a poet. She traveled throughout West and East Germany and went on to publish a special collection of poems in German, largely reflections on and tributes to the unexpected kinship and connection she found with Germans in a time of political turmoil and protest.

> The Left gun
> and the Right gun
> Face the Line.
> tanks wait
> by train tracks
> under the trees.
> leaves listen
> To throbbing hills
> tell legends
> about men
> with double vision –
> wingless Spiders
> who will sacrifice
> ancient
> and injured
> cities.
>
> i hold hands
> with the women.
> we make a ring
> around the children.
> The men plant
> flowers forever
> to never forget.
> In our throats,
> The trigger
> is cocked.[2]

In addition to Wayne State University in Detroit, where she continues to teach, Boyd was a professor at the University of Iowa and Ohio State University and a past director of African American Studies at the University of Michigan-Flint. For 16 years, she was chair of WSU's Department of African American Studies. She earned her doctorate in English from the University of Michigan and her master's and bachelor's degrees from Western Michigan University.

To John Percy Boyd III, Melba's oldest child, the most impressive fact of her life remains what he witnessed growing up. "We traveled the world with her, to Germany and France; we were always going somewhere for some award," he explains. "But the amazing part to me is that she did so much while also being this confident, calm and cool mom."

John and his sister, Maya, were born during Melba's first marriage. "I grew up without a father, but I had a mother who made sure I always had everything I needed to compete and excel in life. I played a lot of sports and she was always there. She would play catch with me. I didn't know that she was big in the world too. I still think of her that way, more as my mom, my rock, than the poet that she is."

The Book of Melba

FACT 3:
Melba the poet does not write pretty poems.

Her essays probe and punch. Even the elegies she creates by request upon the deaths of leaders, legends and loved ones, do not pacify. They roar in remembrance. Melba means to make you hear the lessons of injustice and the work-a-day heroes who in their resistance, their survival, keep culture moving.

there is a sickness
in our time,
a sour toxic virus
infecting our senses,
an evil
more ravenous
than our need
to be sane.
where will it
lead us?
will the strong
overcome or
succumb to the
sacrilege of

Ethnic cleansing, or
Anti-semitism, or
christian racism
or muslim fanaticism, or
fanatic patriotism?

Everyone wants
The right to
Hate,
To be the
biggest voice
Of indignation
On the front
Page of
freedom

of speech,
the united press
of belligerent
Ignorance
Feeding our fear
In the turmoil
Of the millennium.
Will these two-legged
Beasts riding skeletons
Into the maelstrom,
Perish in blue blazers
Ignited by their
Own vengeance?[3]

Those who see mastery in Melba's poems laud her for confronting uncomfortable truths and wrapping them in words that are accessible but rhythmic too.

LEFT Cover from *Letters to Ché.*

RIGHT Cover from *Abandon Automobile: Detroit City Poetry 2001*, edited by Melba and M.L. Liebler.

"I hesitate to use the words 'populist poet,' but that's Melba's mystique, I think," explains the award-winning poet M.L. Liebler, who has published Melba's work and co-edited notable anthologies with her including *Abandon Automobile: Detroit City Poetry 2001*. In the book's preface, Melba makes plain the difference she sees in Detroit poets: "Detroit poets cling to the craziness of resistance in the face of literary traditions, and they scoff at the rules of conventional politics."

Those words fit Melba too. "Her poems speak directly to the people because she's grounded in people, the people of Detroit, and around the world too when you consider she's someone who has taught and read work globally," Liebler continues. "You can hear Melba even if you're not comfortable hearing what she's saying."

> they will never hear
> our words
> gently raving
> in a book.
> scientists don't visit
> poets.
> capitalists don't understand
> esoteric words
> studded with hot ice.
> they live inside fortresses
> hiding under false
> moonscrape umbrellas
>
> today,
> we read
> in the shelter
> of artists;
> a collection of poets,
> a few musicians,
> a quartet of painters —
> a menagerie of
> image makers.
>
> but our choir
> is not big enough.
> we need an explosion!
> running up steps
> climbing throats
> occupying eyes
> talking
> talking
>
> exposing lies[4]

The Book of Melba

FACT 4:
Detroit is Melba's omnipresent muse.

Award-winning jazz bassist Marion Hayden has known Melba for more than two decades. She often accompanies Melba on stage for select poetry readings. Beyond their friendship, Hayden regards Melba as one of Detroit's most devoted arts ambassadors.

"You see Melba around town with all these hats," explains Hayden, a 2016 Kresge Artist Fellow. "To me she really just wears one big one that encompasses this multiverse. You've got poetry in there, cultural writing, film, live performance, a love and understanding of music, and an amazing willingness to be a conduit especially for Detroit. She regales in the people that live here and the kinds of cultural gifts we give, humbly, to the world. We mentor people; we send them out and they remind the world, just as Melba does, what Detroit is about."

Melba explains her love this way: "I think I was really blessed to grow up Black in Detroit," she says. "I've always wanted the broader public to understand how different an experience it was to be surrounded by people, all kinds of people, making culture. And you know, we've been doing it a long time without a lot of major support until recently."

But do not mistake Melba for a myopic or nostalgic civic booster. "As a poet and as a person, she's this wonderful mix of kind and generous," explains fellow writer and long-time friend Nancy Falconer. "But she's also fiercely political and passionate, a passion which came from tragedy." The two met as 15-year-olds in Tobermory, Canada, where their families owned adjacent cottages. "The fire in Melba has never gone out. It's what draws people to her."

Melba's most memorable poems cry out in defiance of oppressive systems and ring with demands of justice, honesty and change.

LEFT Melba performs with longtime friends and award-winning musicians, bassist Marion Hayden and vocalist Shahida Nurullah.

BELOW Melba after a reading at Wayne State University in Detroit.

In signature poems such as *we want our city back, burial of a building* and *this museum was once a dream*, Melba travels through Detroit's history, serenades its heroes and sounds alarms about long-standing horrors. You hear the dismay of the city, across racial lines, when she questions, for instance, the implosion of the famed J.L. Hudson's department store.

> when they bring
> a building down,
> when they make
> history absent,
> when they implode
> a cistern of memories
> into a basement grave,
> where do the
> ghosts go?[5]

In poem after poem, Melba questions the social costs of perennial struggles against blight, disenfranchisement and broken promises of prosperity.

> the corporate state
> measured and
> maneuvered
> the real estate.
> they purchased
> collusion on
> the eve
> of elections
> in private rooms
> where lawyers
> convene with
> judges,
> the lords
> of the discourse
> of dismemberment.

> they protected
> the power
> of wealth
> and the right
> of Americans
> to shop for
> that dream house
> by the river
> with the "Trail
> of Tears" running
> through it[6]

The Book of Melba

FACT 5:
Melba Joyce Boyd merits applause.

She was chosen as the 2023 Kresge Eminent Artist due, in part, to facts 1–4 and the many other details of her life that fill the pages you're about to explore.

Established in 2008 by The Kresge Foundation, the award is now regarded as a coveted mark of lifelong artistic excellence and cultural contribution. The panel of select metro Detroit artists and arts professionals that made the 2023 selection was unanimous. The relevance of Melba's work, they said, continues to withstand time.

"From her work as a poet and a writer to her work as a historian, as an educator, as just so many things, you see the impact, the love she has for the craft and for Detroit and you see why she's deserving," explains panelist, poet and interdisciplinary artist Scheherazade Washington Parrish. "She's exactly an eminent artist."

Grace Serra, Art Collection Curator for Wayne State University, said, "The quality of the work she's done and the continued relevance is important. It's about social justice and honesty. And she's fierce. She hasn't mellowed with age. You can tell there's still more to be said."

At 73, Melba is making plans for more, not less. In 2024, she'll return to the University of Bremen as an Artist-In-Residence. She dreams of bringing the life of abolitionist poet Frances E. W. Harper to film. Her biography of Harper, *Discarded Legacy: Politics and Poetics in the Life of Frances E. W. Harper, 1825–1911* (1994), is widely acclaimed as the first comprehensive study of this major literary figure of the abolitionist and women's rights movements.

But the documentary is just the tip of Melba's creative to-do-one-day list. She talks of venturing into children's literature with her daughter, Maya, an artist and illustrator: a new family legacy to share with her four grandchildren. And there's still much to do to help Detroit and America connect to Randall's legacy too. She envisions finding full financial support to display his library including a public reading room. The collection was donated to

Wayne State University in 2004 but has yet to be unveiled. Also, there's the ongoing question of a Melba memoir: Will she or won't she? Friends, fellow poets, and former students are forever prodding.

"I'm not sitting around thinking a lot about my legacy," she explains, "because, you know, I'm Presbyterian, and the Presbyterians believe this s--- is all predestined anyway. All I know is, the older I get, the more I believe you don't really plan it; you just keep doing the things you love, stay on the path, and things work out."

Nichole M. Christian is a writer and veteran journalist. She is creative director, editor and lead writer of four Kresge Foundation Eminent Artist monographs: *The Culture Keeper* (2022), honoring Olayami Dabls; A *Palette for The People* (2021), honoring painter and educator Shirley Woodson; *Wonder and Flow* (2020), honoring ceramicist Marie Woo; and *A Life Speaks* (2019), honoring poet and activist Gloria House. Nichole is also coauthor of *Canvas Detroit*, and frequent essayist for M Contemporary Art, a gallery in Ferndale, Michigan. She has written for the PBS American Masters Series.

Her writing also appears in the poetry chapbook Cypher, summer 2021; *Portraits 9/11/01: The Collected "Portraits of Grief" from The New York Times*; the online arts journal *Essay'd; A Detroit Anthology*, and *Dear Dad: Reflections on Fatherhood.*

1. Whitman, Walt. "Song of Myself (1892 version) by Walt Whitman." Poetry Foundation, https://www.poetryfoundation.org/poems/45477/song-of-myself-1892.

2. Excerpt, "wingless spiders, Bremen, December 17, 1983", *blues music sky of mourning, the German poems,* Past Tents Press, 2006.

3. Excerpt, "in the absence of meaning", *Letters to Ché,* Poems by Melba Joyce Boyd, Ridgeway Press, 1996.

4. Excerpt, "false moonscape umbrellas, for George Tysh," *the province of literary cats,* Melba Joyce Boyd, Past Tents Press, 2002.

5. Excerpt, "burial of a building, upon the implosion of the J.L. Hudson's Department Store," *the province of literary cats,* Melba Joyce Boyd, Past Tents Press, 2002.

6. Excerpt, "the view of blue", *the province of literary cats,* Melba Joyce Boyd, Past Tents Press, 2002.

Reflections from Melba Joyce Boyd's literary peers, family and friends on her creative and cultural legacy.

Respe

Nichole M. Christian

Portrait of Melba by Maya Wynn Boyd, 2023.

When the Queen of Soul, Aretha Franklin, died in 2018, Melba Joyce Boyd picked up her pen to lend her voice to the legacy of the legendary daughter of Detroit.

The poem titled *Rock Steady for The Queen of Soul* is pure Melba: on beat and Detroit proud. Yet more lurks in its opening lines, an unintended window into some of the city's reverence for the poet's voice too.

In the third stanza, Melba writes,

> "Your songs soar with angels,
> strengthen our resolve,
> demand RESPECT
> like a natural woman
> to THINK, to Do Right
> despite racial strife"[1]

Clearly, it's Aretha that Melba is conjuring. But reread the stanza. Imagine the words "poems" and "Detroit" in place of "songs" and "natural." To reimagine, even playfully, is to tap into what many describe as Melba's singularity, her poetry and her persona.

"There are poets who have a gift of cadence, a gift of making people come to their feet. Melba is that type of poet. She connects to the people," says Charles Ferrell, co-director of the James and Grace Lee Boggs Center in Detroit, who worked with Melba while he was vice president for public programs and community engagement at the Charles H. Wright Museum of African American History. "She has an absolute fire and connection to Detroit, to history. It's important that we honor her service and dedication."

LEFT Maya Boyd and Melba Boyd in Los Angeles in 2010 for the NAACP Image Awards.

RIGHT A selection of the many titles written or edited by Melba Joyce Boyd.

Like many close to Melba, Maya Boyd was thrilled to learn that her mother now joins a select group of 15 creatives — painters, poets, photographers, musicians and others — prized with the Kresge Eminent Artist title and its accompanying acclaim.

Maya, a frequent illustrator of Melba's books and poetry tribute projects, was by her mother's side in Los Angeles in 2010 for the NAACP Image Awards. Melba's book *Roses and Revolution: The Selected Writings of Dudley Randall* had been named a finalist. Though she did not win, she reveled in the national attention and delighted especially in being "styled" for the event by her daughter. "She's always getting some award or some honor for that part of her life," Maya says.

The moment, Maya recalls, was star studded. Yet she believes that the Kresge Eminent Artist Award looms larger.

"People around the world know how much she loves Detroit," says Maya. "She takes the city wherever she goes. But to be recognized at this level, at this time in her life, it's like Detroit saying, 'We see you. We love you back.'"

Maya and her young son, Maverick, are now next-door neighbors to Oma, the German word for grandmother. When John IV was born on March 25, 2009, Melba was in Bremen, Germany, celebrating a friend, Ursula Bauer's birthday. When she got the phone call from her son, everyone shouted in German: "Melba ist eine Oma."

For two decades Maya lived and worked in New York City, despite her mother's insistence that she try life as an artist in Detroit. "My mother has always had more hope than sadness about Detroit," she said. "It's the main reason I came back, for my son to be developed in this community, close to her love and the culture."

  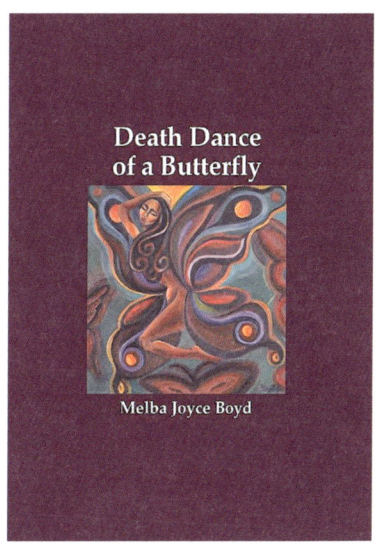

Living next door has also deepened her understanding of Melba's impact as a Detroit-based poet, editor and biographer. "She never stopped believing and being part of what people are now coming to see about the city. She could've been an artist and a teacher anywhere," Maya explains. "But she chose to stay here through a huge span of change, to be a part of it. She's still committed."

Poet Sonya Pouncy can recite verse by verse what she loves about "Melba poems." But poetry alone paints an incomplete picture of Melba's impact, she says.

"When you think about the number of books that she's published but also the number of poets, like me, whose work she's introduced as an editor or all that's she done as a professor, you're talking about tremendous, and really layered unsung impact on the art and in individuals' lives."

Pouncy points to her writing life as an example. "I've been published in at least two or three anthologies, and I've been able to perform the work of Frances Harper, all because of Melba's encouragement and her endorsements. She's truly taken a cue from her mentor, Dudley, in that way," says Pouncy.

"The next generation of poets is always top of mind for her: Who will be our voices next? Let's see what they have to say now and how I can help? That's Melba for you, and it's what makes her legacy so much bigger than if she were only making and sharing her poems."

Melba's poems and essays mix biting social critique with an insider's reverence for Detroit history and cultural traditions. At her core, Melba is a writer energized by the art of remembrance even when it's personally painful.

Petals Like Blades

A twin love of family and words is what pulled Melba through "a tragedy in my personal life that I could not have imagined in my worst nightmare."

In December of 1972, one of Melba's brothers, 23-year-old Vietnam veteran John Percy Boyd Jr., an 18-year-old cousin Hayward Brown, and their friend Mark Bethune, 22, were in a shootout with police. That incident eventually led to the end of the most violent chapters of policy harassment and brutality in Detroit's history.

The three young Black men engaged in a shootout with four white Detroit police officers outside a reputed drug house. The officers were assigned to the city's controversial undercover Stop the Robberies, Enjoy Safe Streets (STRESS) unit. Melba's brother and the two others were members of an underground "vigilante" group determined to force drug dealers out of Black neighborhoods. The four officers were all seriously wounded. A second shootout between police and the trio later that month left one officer dead and another critically wounded.

The manhunt for Boyd, Brown, and Bethune — as recounted in an online University of Michigan HistoryLab project — led to "extraordinary abuses of the civil and constitutional rights of hundreds of Black citizens and the killing of an innocent man during one of many warrantless home invasions." Large-scale protests from across the Black community followed.

Two months later, after Brown had been apprehended in Detroit, Melba's brother John and Bethune were tracked to Atlanta. They were with Melba's half-brother Owen Darnell Winfield, who lived in the city. Both brothers were killed by police in the manhunt she writes about in "In Hot Pursuit: The Deadly Consequences of Detroit Police Oppression," an essay published in The Journal of Law in Society and in *Wrestling with the Muse*. The deaths of Melba's brothers and Bethune – who reportedly took his own life after being wounded by police – made national headlines.

LEFT Melba's brother, John Percy Boyd, Jr.
RIGHT Melba's half-brother, Owen Darnell Winfield.

"I got the news of my brothers' deaths after returning to Detroit from a poetry festival at Central Michigan University," Melba recalled. She had been in the company of a coterie of rising Black literary stars, including Quincy Troupe and Alice Walker, who would go on to become the first Black woman to win a Pulitzer Prize for Literature. She immediately sent Melba a copy of her famous Broadside publication, "Revolutionary Petunias." Walker wrote: "Melba, May your petals grow like blades of steel to protect you."

When Melba returned to work at Broadside Press, she shared the poem she had written for her brothers' funeral with Dudley Randall. He insisted that it be published in the iconic Broadside series.

Detroit police during the manhunt. Detroit Free Press archives.

Broadside Series
No. 68

TO DARNELL AND JOHNNY
(February 23, 1973)

Owen Darnell Winfield, born May 22, 1945 and John Percy Boyd, Jr., born January 2, 1949, were assasinated by an agent of the State while struggling for Black Liberation—
"Africa will rise."

I will always remember
how much life
is you.
your smiles
could cure with bright
stars of laughter.

I will always remember
how much life
is you.
your strength
could hug and protect
with peace giving arms.

I will always remember
how much love
is your life.
giving them for
tomorrow's children
of the universe.

I will always remember,
and you will always live
in the Spirit of the New World,
you helped to build.

    Love,
        your sister
        Melba

Broadside No. 68, Broadside Series
February, 1973
Copyright © 1973 by Melba J. Boyd
All Rights Reserved
First and only Broadside printing of 500 copies
Broadside Press, 12651 Old Mill Place, Detroit, Michigan 48238

The reverberations of the incidents played a key role in the 1973 Detroit mayoral election when the anti-STRESS Michigan State Sen. Coleman A. Young prevailed against the Detroit Police Commissioner John Nichols who had presided over the hunt for the men he labeled as "Mad Dog Killers."

While the tragedy is now looked upon as painful history, Sandra Boyd, Melba's sister, awaits the day that Melba will have the final say on the deaths of their older brothers. "There's been some writing here and there, but I've been waiting for Melba to tell the whole story," says Sandra, a retired math and computer science teacher. "I used to bug her about when. Then I stopped. I said, well, she's an artist, it has to come when she's ready."

But unlike others, Sandra, who is two years younger than Melba, is certain Melba's memoir will happen and be a "correct" retelling of family tragedy and truth. "It doesn't consume us anymore, and Melba's writing has certainly grown, but we still talk about our brothers. That tight legacy, and what we went through is what I think people will appreciate when her memoir comes. It's just a matter of time."

OPPOSITE Anti-STRESS flyer, Roman S. Gribbs Mayoral Records, Burton Historical Collection, Detroit Public Library.

Legacy and Lore

Semaj Brown is Flint, Michigan's, first poet laureate. But she was born in Detroit, a native of Conant Gardens, the same historic neighborhood where Melba and her brothers grew up.

 "I was a little girl, but I heard my mother always talking about her, talking about what happened to her brother and how horrible it was. Even though they weren't still living in Conant Gardens by that time, there was this lore about her and her family," Brown said.

Brown met Melba years later while she was a student at Wayne State University and Melba was a visiting writer. "I heard the name Boyd, and said, Oh, my God! That's the lady they had been talking about all along," says Brown.

When Melba published the biography of Dudley Randall, Brown celebrated by buying copies for elders in Conant Garden, who, like her mother, remembered Melba. "Everybody was so proud of how she stood up and what she became," says Brown. "She has this legacy, and it's just beautiful to see how she's lived it and shared it."

 For Brown, Melba epitomizes the role of the poet in society. "Poetry is not supposed to be about celebrities. Poetry is about having a voice for the voiceless; it's about speaking truth to power, speaking truth to yourself, saying things in a way that people hear it different for the first time," she says.

MAD DOG KILLERS!!

Before the Black community goes off half-cocked as to the reasons why these STRESS Storm-Troopers along with the rest of the Detroit Police Department are kicking down doors, threatening and killing anyone who comes between them and their prey Mark Bethune, John Percy Boyd, and Hayward Brown, we should first understand some things.

First we should not assume as police commissioner John Nichols seems to have done that the men Mark Bethune, John Percy Boyd, and Hayward Brown committed these crimes or for that matter, are anyway connected with them. THIS MUST BE PROVEN IN A COURT OF LAW, NOT A T.V. PRESS CONFERENCE.

Secondly, we should not assume that the information we receive from the news media is correct, especially since we have only heard one side. STRESS's side.

We do not really know if the men who are accussed of killing these STRESS officers were fired on first or not. Therefore, we do not know if they were acting in self defense or not. This can only be brought out in a court of law.

As of now, since their guilt has not been proven in a court of law "we of the Black community demand an immediate apology from Commissioner John Nichols for calling our sons, brothers, and husbands MAD DOG KILLERS. We will except nothing less than a televised apology NOW!

Who's calling whom "Mad Dog Killers"
We know who the real Mad Dogs are!!

Its a matter of life...Stop STRESS
SAVE THE CHILDREN::: STOP STRESS

SAVE YOUR INNOCENT LIVES...SAVE YOUR
INNOCENT LIVES...STOP STESSS

"People from Melba's generation, particularly her, understand that on a very innate level, I think, because of the struggles they had to go through to become recognized writers, to become professors, just to survive."

Literary Kin

Don't ask acclaimed poet, editor, and biographer Quincy Troupe how long he's known Melba or exactly how they first met. Those details pale in relevance to the facts that have made Troupe a champion of Melba's work and cemented a lasting literary kinship.

"I've known Melba for so many years I cannot remember. I think I met her when she was working with Dudley at Broadside Press," recalls Troupe, who lives in New York and is most celebrated as the biographer of jazz giant Miles Davis. "She's always invited me to participate in all kinds of readings and artist residency programs in Detroit. She's always treated me with the utmost kindness and respect, which I have tried my best to return in equal measure. My wife Margaret and I consider her one of our very best friends."

Troupe, who is also a professor emeritus at the University of California, San Diego, in La Jolla, traces his high regard for Melba to her deep commitment to cultural preservation. "Melba is the consummate scholar, the keeper of traditions and the legacy of African American literature, arts and culture. Her poetry is steeped in the blues and classical African American sentiment and expression."

He adds: "She has been the driving force behind everything literary in Detroit for more than half a century. She is absolutely respected for her own writing, for her views on racial or social justice issues, women's issues, the African American aesthetic, or the political landscape in these still yet-to-be-United States. Melba is a formidable, committed academic, professor, and artist."

Force in Her Voice

Frank Rashid, a former professor emeritus of English at Detroit's Marygrove College, has never forgotten his first encounter with Melba Joyce Boyd. She was young. He was too. The year was 1974.

"I didn't know anything about her then," he recalls. Rashid was working as a volunteer for WDET, Detroit's public radio station, helping to capture the public hearing surrounding the city's controversial STRESS police unit. "There were so many people who needed to be at that hearing that they moved it from the City County Building to Ford Auditorium, which held several thousand people. We were broadcasting because it was such an important moment in the life of the city."

When Melba took the mic, Rashid was riveted. "I saw this young woman get up and passionately speak about her brother, his friend, and her cousin, and what was going on and the injustice to them and so many. She had a fire and a force in her voice that you never forget. You could hear her anger and this brilliance."

Years later, through a shared connection to Dudley Randall, they became collaborators, friends and co-creators of a series of literary events celebrating the friendship and legacies of Randall and legendary Detroit poet Robert Hayden. Hayden was the first African American to be appointed as Consultant in Poetry to the U.S. Library of Congress.

Working closely with Melba, Rashid was often reminded of that first encounter. "I began to put it all together, to understand the source of the strength that you experience in so many of her poems. She expresses such a knowledge and appreciation of Detroit, and the legacy of loss. The reason that she's such a force is because she's lived the city's history. She's someone you want to listen to and learn from."

She Was Black Like Me

Opal Moore didn't know much about Melba Joyce Boyd when they met in the 1980s except that she was a poet from Detroit, a published author and a woman bold enough to bring her brand of Blackness to the predominantly white University of Iowa. For Moore, a Black graduate student in the English department, those few details were reasons enough to rejoice about the new faculty candidate.

"In those days, there were not very many Black people applying into these universities, and here she was walking in with, as far as I was concerned, an archive of history that the University of Iowa's English department needed desperately to acquire."

As Moore remembers, rumors of Melba's application were running wild with excitement among grad students, partly because she was Black and well published, compared to the buzz about another applicant, someone "straight out of graduate school, who didn't have any book publications."

Moore recalls Melba bringing a distinctly confident and unapologetically Black persona to the largely white campus. She stood out. "What I learned watching her had to do with how she entered." To Moore, Melba's commitment to full cultural representation is an important embodiment of the main lesson from author Anna Julia Cooper's seminal 'When and Where I enter... race enters with me.'[3]

Years later as an associate professor of English at Spelman College in Atlanta, Georgia, Moore regularly exposed her students to Melba's writing, often inviting her to campus and publishing her poetry in *Aunt Chloe,* the college's literary journal. Today, Moore, who is retired, also counts Melba as a friend.

"Melba is a cultural treasure. She has immersed her creative energy in ways that link to the community rather than objectifying it as a point of study. The clarity of that vision about why it is you're doing the work that you do and what compels you is critical. She could be anywhere, but she's at Wayne State University for a very clear set of articulable reasons.''

In fact, Moore says Melba's real cultural impact is beyond her work with words. "The way to regard Melba Joyce Boyd is to regard the whole of her practice. She embodies something that we don't want to lose in the way that we think about Black artists and women artists, and scholar artists. Sometimes they go into the academy and parts of who they are disappear. It's not the case with Melba. She has made her art useful in the African tradition where your art is an expression of spirit and connection.''

Wholly Melba

In Melba's life, Sandra Ware wears the best friend badge. They met at Pershing High School in the 1960s, well before Melba had any interest or inkling of a life lived as an award-winning writer and future distinguished professor. In those days, she was Melba the cheerleader, the athlete and doting younger sister to "Johnny.''

The signs of who Melba would become were always present, says Ware, a retired psychiatric therapist.

"She's always been the high-achiever, gifted with words, sensitive, highly intuitive to the rhythms of cultures, ethnicities, and their beginnings. She's a born leader, compassionate and strong in her convictions in life and in writing.''

While Ware, who is also the godmother to Melba's two children, has "loved'' watching Melba's long record of academic and artistic achievements, what she prizes most about her friend is a telling personal quality.

"It's hard to explain, but if you look in Melba's eyes, she has this glimmering soulfulness that tells you she's a thinker, always studying but there's calmness in her strength. I think that's what draws people to her in life and to her work. She came out of chaos and she honestly wants you to believe you will also come out of whatever chaos you face, and also standing on your feet."

In September of 2019, Ware faced the toughest moment of her life. An ailing sister died suddenly. Within 24 hours, Ware's mother, who had seemed to accept the news of her daughter's death, sat down in her chair and she died.

"I went into a fog, just this total zombie. Nothing seemed real. I have this vague memory of my mother's body being removed and looking across the room, and somehow Melba was there. From then on, she remained at my side, and she calmly and serenely helped to bring a surreal, horrendous nightmare to a sacred memory."

To Ware, Melba Joyce Boyd is best measured by her constancy of care and commitment to community. "This is her foundation; this is her innards; this is what she bred up for. She has never stopped showing up. This is what one should respect about Melba. Her life, not the books; that's her art."

1. Excerpt, Rock Steady for The Queen of Soul, 2019 broadside, Past Tents Press.

2. Broadside No. 68, Broadside Series, February 1973, copyright by Melba J. Boyd, All Rights Reserved, First and only Broadside Press, Detroit.

3. When and Where I Enter: Anna Julia Cooper, Afrocentric Theory, and Africana Studies. LaRese C. Hubbard, Journal of Black Studies, Vol. 40, No. 2 (Nov., 2009).

Sound Stories
Listen along to Melba as she reflects on her roots, family, and rise in the literary world.

We invite you to listen along as Melba shares personal stories about some of her life's major influences, contained as audio stories and accessible via QR codes throughout the book. Audio produced by Zak Rosen.

Her Words

In Her Own Words:

Roots

Melba Joyce Boyd reflects on her parents' defining choice to leave behind multigenerational roots in Alabama for the promise of prosperity in Detroit.

To preserve the organic nature of the conversation we have chosen to omit the traditional question-and-answer format.

The Book of Melba

ABOVE   Melba as a young child.

RIGHT   Melba shares a photo of her father during his time in the military.

PREVIOUS   Melba as a girl; a family portrait; a young Melba with her mother Dorothy and younger sister Sandra.

we did not grow
between concrete
cracks like weeds in
an asphalt jungle
we were planted
by parents[1]

—Melba Joyce Boyd

I grew up in *south* southwest Detroit, like way southwest, almost out of the city. You say southwest and most people think you're talking about Mexicantown.[2] No, no, no. I mean so far out there you could walk across the city line by passing three streets from River Rouge into Ecorse.

That neighborhood was developed during that Second Great Migration[3] and, during and after World War II, a place for Black workers to live so they wouldn't try to move into Dearborn. Any children of white people still living in our neighborhood went to St. Andrew and Benedict Catholic schools. When you study housing discrimination in Detroit, restrictive covenants were also applied against Catholics and Jews.

We lived at 2433 Deacon St. It was just a little two bedroom bungalow, but my father maximized the space. He finished the attic so my two older brothers could have the big bedroom up there.

Later, when my oldest brother Darnell moved out and was in the Marines, my sister and I got the big bedroom. My brother John had to take the smaller room where we were. My father finished the basement too. It wasn't big but it was nice.

My dad had been in the Army. He bought the house with the GI Bill. A lot of the young men on that street had been in the service like my dad. After he got out, he went back to Alabama to finish college. In fact, if he had not gone to the war, and then gone back to school, he and my mom probably would have missed each other because my mom was still finishing high school when he got drafted. They met at Tuskegee University. If not for the draft, he would have graduated in '45, before she ever went to college. She didn't enter Tuskegee until 1946. They definitely would've missed each other, and I probably wouldn't be here.

The Book of Melba

I'm not a hundred percent sure which side of my family came to Detroit first. The Boyds came at the beginning of WWII like a lot of Black families from the South. On the Wynn side, my Aunt Odessa and her husband, Peter Brown, came during that time as well. Uncle Pete came about that time. Her husband worked at the Ford Rouge Plant, building tanks. My father's mother, Bernice Boyd, had been a school teacher in Selma. In Detroit, she worked for the U.S. government at the U.S. Armory. It paid better than teaching elementary school in Alabama.

My grandmother had three sisters, who all came to Detroit during WWII. Both sides of my family were chasing the same dream, same promise.

My father graduated with a degree in mechanical engineering in 1948 from Tuskegee University. After the war, there was a lot of talk about new opportunities, so he expected to work as an engineer.

But he would never get to pursue this career. When he interviewed, a personnel manager at Ford told him, "You're more than qualified, but we don't hire colored engineers." What they meant by "colored" was anyone Black, Brown or Asian; they were only hiring White engineers.

So, my dad ended up working at the main post office downtown, which used to be called the Black graduate school because the discrimination prevented most educated Black people from practicing their degrees. Daddy started as a clerk and eventually became a supervisor. It was a good paying job like working in the factory, but not brutal or as dangerous. I'll never forget what that did to my dad.

My son, John Boyd III, has the same degree, from the University of Michigan, just in a different era and he works as an engineering consultant for NASCAR companies.

Melba shares family photos in her home in Detroit.

OPPOSITE Melba's maternal grandparents Sarah and Owen Wynn in approximately 1930; Bessemer, Alabama.

For both of my parents, education was a strong family value, especially on my dad's side, going back several generations. I'm third generation; maybe even the fourth to graduate from college. The further you go back though, it gets really interesting. It's something that I still need to research. My grandfather's oldest sister, Inez Boyd Fosten, she was a professor at Tennessee State. My grandfather Richard Boyd attended Alabama State University, and that's where he met Bernice — my grandmother. That's partly why education was so important to my dad. It's a deep legacy.

My mom's family, on the other hand, was different. They were from Bessemer, Alabama. Her parents, Sarah and Owen Wynn, probably only had an eighth grade education. During the early nineteenth century, high school was not readily available for most Black children. But, they believed in education and sending their children to college, so they would acquire a professional degree and become economically independent.

I do know that Granddaddy Wynn was a big labor advocate, and he was a supervisor of Black workers in the ore mines in Bessemer. He made a good living, and invested in property and education for his children. My grandmother grew crops for sale and maintained a family garden. They both agreed that the children — 13 girls and one boy — should go to college, especially the girls so that they'd be able to take care of themselves instead of depending on a man. They invested in that belief, which was very progressive at the time.

Growing up, one of the funniest stories I heard about my granddaddy was his response to some man who said to him one day at church, "Why you sending those girls to college? They ain't gonna do nothing but get married." My grandfather, who was a deacon in the church, said to him: "Mind your own damn business."

I think the story also explains much about their family values and about misperceptions a lot of people had, and still have, about Black people in the South during the 19th and 20th centuries.

The Book of Melba

Sound Story No. 1
Melba reflects on the legacy of the daring abolitionist poet Frances Harper.

They weren't just walking around with their heads down. The truth is you had a lot of Black folks in those times who were progressive. It's the same kind of thinking that Frances Harper was advocating with her writing and speaking to groups after slavery: this idea that they had to learn to read and write in order to become self-sufficient. Even with 14 children, my grandparents were forward thinking, serious about it, too. They knew they had to be for their children.

My dad was rather quiet and reserved. He taught me how to read and do math at age four. My mom was very assertive and expressive. I think it was necessary for a Black woman of her generation. She loved swimming, and when she was a senior in high school, she went to the Recreation Department for the City of Bessemer and asked: "When do the colored kids get to swim in the pool at the recreation center?" It's 1945.

He responded with: "When you get a colored life guard."

Next year, my mom goes to Tuskegee University, majors in physical education, gets her lifeguard certification, returns to the Recreation Department the following summer, and tells the man: "We got a colored life guard now." For my mom, this was about fairness. When her father and her older brother taught her how to swim, they had to go to a nearby creek and beat snakes out of the water, so it would be safe to get in the water. So, she thought, why are we swimming in the creek? We should be swimming in the city pool.

I think it speaks to this very strong sense of integrity and identity. She told me once that her father taught his children at an early age that nobody is better than you; but also, you're no better than anyone else. That stuck with her. In a lot of Black families you see these patterns, these values, that get instilled early and they get passed down.

ABOVE   Family photo of Melba's mother Dorothy, top right, her maternal grandmother Sarah Wynn and 11 of the 14 Wynn siblings.

RIGHT   Melba's great-grandmother Taylor.

LEFT   Melba's great-grandfather Percy Smith.

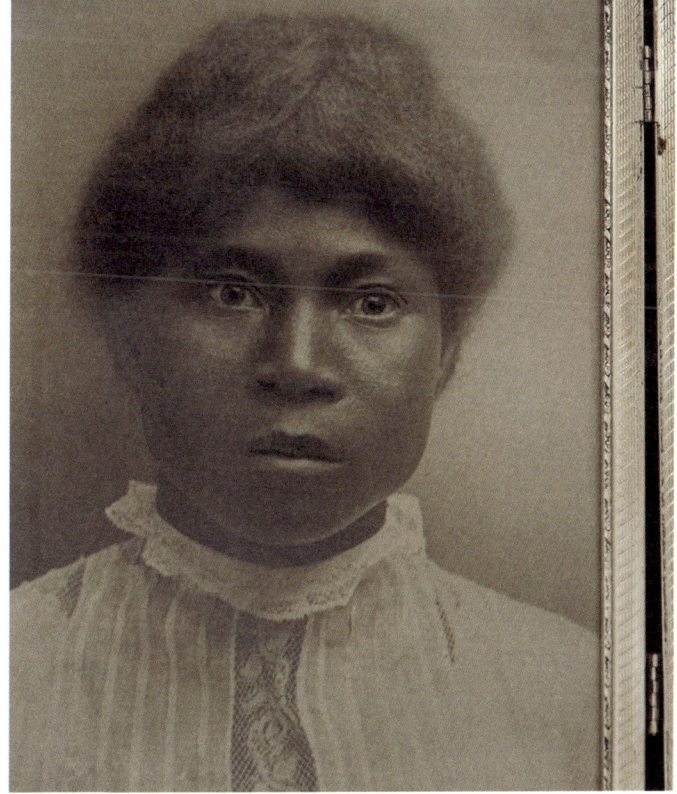

The Book of Melba

Sound Story No. 2
Melba recalls the sounds that enlivened her Detroit upbringing.

I am the oldest daughter of six children and the oldest of the four still living.

My older brothers, Darnell and John, are deceased. I've written about their deaths and will write more extensively about them in my memoirs. I don't think I'll ever stop processing that trauma and tragedy. I miss them every day.

But I also remember just growing up with normal moments of being a kid, feeling very peaceful in the yard, playing ball with my brothers, Johnny and Darnell, and with my sister, Sandy. I remember the trees. There were many in the neighborhood, lining the streets, proving shade and oxygen. My dad planted a peach tree that actually bore fruit, and one of my brother's friends, Ron Watters, who lived down the street, had several fruit trees in his yard. For the most part, our parents were southern immigrants, who knew how to grow trees and to tend gardens with flowers and food. They continued these practices when they settled in Detroit.

In retrospect, as a child, I was not affected by historical events impacting the nation or the world. I grew up with a secure sense of a community that was solid and stable. For the most part, families were financially secure. You knew your neighbors and they knew you. I felt safe.

My parents divorced when I was about 15. They sold the house and my mother remarried. My father was still a father in my life. He paid child support and we visited him often; he and my step-father, Siegel Clore II, were very similar in temperament and had real respect for each other because they were men both WWII veterans, college-educated, and who had dealt with all kinds of ridiculous discrimination because of their race. Often, we were in the same spaces, as a family. It never really felt odd because the values we all shared, what their parents gave them and what they gave us: a real strong belief in family.

TOP Melba sorts through generations of family photos with grandson Maverick.

BOTTOM-LEFT Melba and brother John Percy Boyd Jr., approximately 1951.

BOTTOM-RIGHT Melba with her brother John Percy Boyd Jr. and youngest sister Sandra Boyd, in 1972.

The Book of Melba

Sound Story No. 3
Travel with Melba as she revisits how a little known slice of Canada on the Georgian Bay became both a creative muse and a source of rejuvenation for generations of her family.

LEFT Melba's family cottage in Tobermory, ON; Melba (far left) in the water in Tobermory with her youngest sisters Dorothy Donise Davis, center, Sandra Boyd, right, longtime friend Nancy Falconer, and son John Percy Boyd III.

BELOW Siegel Clore II, Melba's stepfather. He began the family's tradition of owning property and vacationing in Tobermory, ON.

1. Excerpted from "the rose in the garden," by Melba Joyce Boyd, *The Province of Literary Cats,* 2002, Past Tents Press.

2. Southwest Detroit's Mexicantown neighborhood has been home to Mexican and Latino immigrants since the 1920s due to the area's proximity to industrial jobs including work at Ford Motor Company.

3. During the Second Great Migration (1940–1970) an estimated 4.3 million Black people migrated north from southern U.S. states such as Alabama.

The Book of Melba

In Her Own Words:

Rise

Melba Joyce Boyd reflects on finding her voice, a trailblazing mentor and an unexpected place amid the Black Arts Movement and Detroit's simultaneous racial justice protests.

To preserve the organic nature of the conversation we have chosen to omit the traditional question-and-answer format.

I held poetry in such reverence that I never thought I could publish any of my own

—Melba Joyce Boyd

The Book of Melba

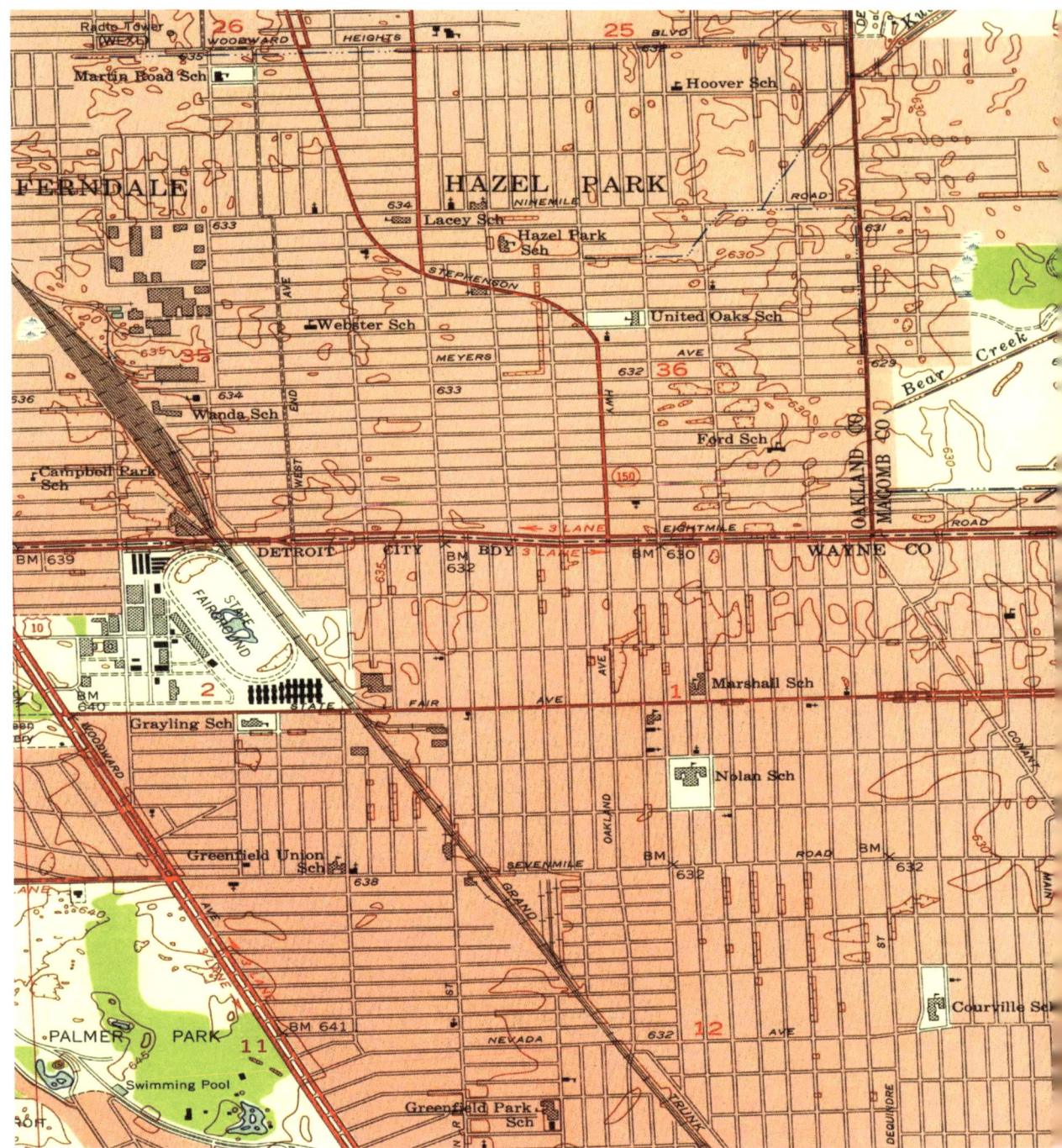

ON P. 60 Melba with her mother Dorothy Clore during a moment at the family cottage Tobermory, Canada.

ON P. 61 Abolitionist poet Frances E. W. Harper, as pictured in Melba's home.

ABOVE A 1968 map of Detroit shows Conant Gardens and surrounding areas, including Pershing High School, where Boyd graduated in 1967.

OPPOSITE Melba poses with her Pershing High School cheerleading squad (5th from left).

After my parents divorced, and my mother remarried, we moved to Conant Gardens,[1] a neighborhood that was essentially developed on land that was granted to Black people to develop housing by Conant, the abolitionist.

At the time we moved, it was a pretty close-knit community, the kind of Black neighborhood in Detroit where your neighbors literally become your extended family, especially when the kids get fused together as friends. We also acquired another brother, John Clore, who was between me and my brother, John Boyd, in age. One of our really good friends to this day is Alex Luvall. We met him the minute we moved. He became friends with me and my brothers. We lived two streets away from each other, and he would be at our house all the time because he only had a much older sister, but no other siblings.

We hung out together, and we got in trouble together, which you never wanted to do because my mom would yell at you, condemn you, and leave you trembling. She would also scold Alex, but not as harshly, saying: "I'm talking to you too, Alex."

I preferred my stepfather's style of parenting; everybody did because he never raised his voice. He would give you this philosophical, global perspective of the consequences to certain actions. I remember one time we'd done something, and Alex was trying to slip out the side door. My stepfather told him to sit down. Certain communities in Detroit are like an extended family. We have deep sense of responsibility for one another, and you feel it.

The Book of Melba

'I Understand Your Concern'

Western Herald

'Go to Hell, Honkies'

VOLUME 52   TUESDAY, APRIL 9, 1968   NUMBER 75

Black vs. University In 8 Hour Stand-off

Make Six Demands of U.

By DAVID McKAY
News Editor

Black students here entered the University Student Center, Friday, April 5, and held it against White intrusion for eight hours.

The demonstrators, claiming to be in mourning over the assassination of Dr. Martin Luther King, Jr., who died of a gunshot wound the night before, entered the center and chained the main doors. Signs were carried or attached bearing such slogans as "The King is Dead—Peace is Also Dead," "We must move from resistance to agggression, From revolt to Revolution," "Honky, are you human?" and "Who's the peacemaker now, Honkies?"

Dr. James W. Miller, president of the university, saw some of the Black students enter the center at about 6:30 a.m. while walking his dogs.

It was learned that many of the women in the demonstration had taken 6:15 a.m. sign-outs from their residence halls, and the center had been effectively taken over by 6:30 a.m. It was not long before White students formed a crowd in front of the center, some opposing the take over, others simply curious.

Shortly after 8:00, the crowd was sizeable enough to be seen from the East Campus. Some spectators were in sympathy with the Black students, also lamenting the death of Dr. King. One White woman in the crowd was overheard as saying, "Dr. King was a real ———head, that's all I can say."

"But," said a White man next to her, "this is the thing he didn't want."

Shortly after 10 a.m., President Miller walked from his offices in the Administration Building to the front steps of the Student Center and delivered two prepared statements to the demonstrators and the spectators. In the first, he described the sorrow with which he viewed the death of "this distinguished theologian, gentleman of thought, and leader for non-violent action."

The second statement came as a result of the Black occupation of the Student Center. In it he described the move as "certainly not in keeping with the principles of Dr. Martin Luther King. What is now being done is a disservice to the memory of Dr. King." He added that classes would be held as usual and the hope that the Black students would "return the Center to its normal use, hopefully immediately." He then passed copies of the statements through the doors held slightly open by the students inside.

Dr. Miller, aside from his prepared statements, sympathized with the demonstration as a memorial for Dr. King. "You are understandably troubled, understandably wanting to do something," he told the crowd, as he offered to hold memorial services for the assassinated Negro leader.

In an attempt to retain calmness and order, Dr. Miller told the White crowd, "You can do the greatest for all of us, if you'll quietly disperse." He added, "I cannot, will not, command you."

A significant side to the entire days proceedings was Dr. Miller's absolute refusal to use any outward show of force. "I have faith and confidence in our people," he said. He promised that there would be no force "unless there's . . . inhumanity to men."

"I've never brought any police on this campus." He closed his talk in front of the Center with "You've (the students) had seven and a half years' experience with me. If that doesn't build up enough faith . . ." He quickly left for his office in the Administration Building.

Following Dr. Miller's statements, the suggestion was made that classes be called to memorialize Dr. Martin Luther King. Though Dr. Miller had said in his official statement that classes would remain in session, there were those in the crowd who felt that calling classes would be a fitting tribute to Dr. King. The suggestion was met with mixed emotions from the crowd, composed totally of Whites. "There's something constructive," said one in the crowd when it was suggested that they go to the President's office to ask for cancellation of all university classes.

Meanwhile, Denny Gadwa, a WMU senior, told the spectators of a memorial service in Kanley Chapel and a memorial march to be made to Bronson Park. Marchers would meet Kalamazoo College students there to hold a service in memory of Dr. King. A few of the students left for the Sangren parking lot to await the beginning of the march.

In the President's offices, all was a confused mixture of ringing telephones and people asking to see the various members of Dr. Miller's staff. The largest contingent was a group of about fifty students asking to see the President about cancellation of classes. They were directed to one of the large conference rooms to wait until he finished a telephone conversation.

The group waited what they thought to be a reasonable length of time before re-entering the President's offices. There they talked with Dr. Miller. He flatly refused to call classes, asking them to wait until funeral arrangements were made for the dead civil rights leader.

Against the argument about repercussions for cutting classes, Dr. Miller answered with a challenge for the students to answer "your conscience," before they act. "If I were at Amherst (where he earned his B.A.) and I felt this way about it, my conscience wouldn't let me stay." He held

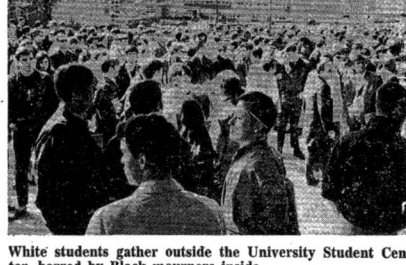
White students gather outside the University Student Center, barred by Black mourners inside.

fast on his decision against cancellation.

While President Miller answered requests for cancellation of classes, a buffer of faculty members lead by Dr. Milton Greenberg, President of the Faculty Senate, began to form between the main doors of the Center and the White spectators on the sidewalk. Several Whites had gone through Spau Tower asking for faculty support of the demonstration and memorial cancellation of classes.

According to Dr. John Phillips, English, the faculty members were there, "simply to provide a buffer between the Black students and action from the outside." Dr. Phillips is also chairman of the Community Relations Board of Kalamazoo, and a past president of the Faculty Senate.

Through this buffer, President Miller entered the Center to talk with the Black students. When he returned, he explained to the spectators that he had six demands outlined by the occupants of the Center. They were:

1. That classes be cancelled for a day.

2. That Dr. Miller issue a statement admitting that the White community has not done its part to help the Blacks.

3. That no retaliatory action be taken by the university against the Black students.

4. That the Student Center close for the day.

5. That four Black students be sent to the King funeral from this university.

6. That the racist curricula be examined at WMU.

President Miller then left the Center to decide on his official reply to the demands.

At about 11 a.m., a memorial march started near Kanley Chapel and ended in Bronson Park, downtown. About 400 students, mostly White, made the march from the Chapel, where a short service had been held with about 150 participants, four of which were Black.

In Bronson Park, a memorial service was held with participants from Kalamazoo College and WMU, officiated by clerical leaders from both schools.

At about the same time, one student among the White spectators in front of the Center suggested, "Let's leave. If we leave, we stand a good chance of having our union back by tonight or tomorrow." This was met by applause from the students and faculty.

Through the crowd and faculty buffer walked five Black women, carrying placards reading "Go to Hell, Honkies!" and "For a taste of Black triumph—Black Power." They were unhindered by any of the whites.

At 2, Dr. Miller left his office for the Student Center. He entered and talked with the Black students. It was announced that he would make an official statement in Kanley Square after talking with the building's occupants.

(Continued on Page 8)

Students hear Dr. Miller's concessions to the Black mourners' six demands.

Memorial services were held in Bronson Park last Friday by WMU and Kalamazoo College students.

Dr. James W. Miller
—Herald photos by Ramsey

Page 1 of the Western Herald, Western Michigan University's student-run newspaper, on Tuesday, April 9, 1968. From the Western Herald archives.

Alex's mother, Mrs. Luvall, was actually the first person to introduce me to the poetry of Robert Hayden[2] and Dudley Randall. My mother was a phys-ed teacher so the books in our library at home were history and politics and whatever but not literature. Mrs. Luvall was an elementary teacher. She had literature in their home and she shared it with me. She was offering me something that I would not get at home and I really didn't realize how much of an influence it would later have. Dudley and Hayden were part of the labor movement in the '30s. They were writing poetry with impact. I just didn't know it yet.

I graduated June of 1967 from Pershing High School. The Detroit Rebellion erupted in July. In the fall, I went to Western (Michigan University) and the following spring, King is assassinated, two days after my 18th birthday. Then, that same year, Bobby Kennedy was killed. I actually shook his hand when he was campaigning in Kalamazoo and spoke near campus.

So, I was so confounded, thinking that this is what adult life is gonna be like, just nonstop intensity. Everything felt like it was connected to the Civil Rights Movement, the Anti-War Movement, and all of it was happening at the same time and in front of our eyes, even at Western. People always think about Ann Arbor as being progressive during the '60s, but things were happening in Kalamazoo too.

After Martin Luther King was assassinated we had a student protest. We called ourselves BAM, the Black Students Action Movement. We occupied the Student Center Building. I was pledging Alpha Kappa Alpha Sorority and it was "Hell Week," the last week of pledging. But Hell Week was disrupted because it was a real hell week with the death of King. When progressive professors and the Students for a Democratic Society (SDS) heard that we were protesting, they formed a barrier outside the building entrance, between us and the state police.

It was really tripped out, something you'd expect to see in Detroit, not in Kalamazoo. We did it because it was necessary.

Sound Story No. 4
Listen to Melba reflect on author James Baldwin's early influence on her writing.

The funny part is I wasn't supposed to go to Western. My mom wanted me to go to Spelman in Atlanta, and my step-dad offered to buy me a car if I stayed home and went to Wayne State. The basic condition was that I could pick either an HBCU or a state school because, even though we were technically middle class, they couldn't afford to send me as well as the rest of my siblings to some elite institution. I knew I didn't want to go down South. I probably would've been in jail with all that was happening there; I mean we're talking about Atlanta in the '60s. I also didn't want to go to University of Michigan or Michigan State because they were both so big. Western was perfect because I wanted to feel like I was really going away and I convinced my best friends at the time, Alex and Sandra, to go with me. They were preparing to go to Wayne State, but I talked them into Western. Sandra's mother, Mrs. Overstreet, drove us to orientation that summer; we were three amigos on our college adventure.

When I started at Western for undergrad, I was a Physical Education major with a dance emphasis. I had studied the arts growing up, including dance and music before college. I played the clarinet in elementary and high school.

But then, I took the freshman composition course, and I just really opened up. I was introduced to James Baldwin, and his words exhilarated my writing. Professor Fritscher suggested I change my major. I wondered if I should do this. I had encouragement from English teachers in high school, especially Ms. Leona Brodsky. I was a good writer, but I didn't think I could become one. But he thought that I had talent. His encouragement and James Baldwin's literature changed my life. I still credit them for this.

Baldwin freed me from the idea that I had to write short sentences because I used to write long ones, and only one or two of my teachers in high school didn't have a problem with that. But the way Baldwin wrote these extended and elegant sentences blew me away. He was also writing about our circumstances. So, that was freedom too, the freedom to write about injustice, and real issues. My parents were cool with me changing majors. They didn't care what I majored in, as long as I studied.

James Baldwin in 1965. Photo by Maria Austria, the Joods Historisch Museum.

I was awarded a MLK Graduate Scholarship to Western, and pursued a master's degree in English. That's when I ran into resistance for the first time. When we had our student demonstration after King was killed, one of our demands was for a Center for Black Studies. During the course, I encountered hostility with Professor Mueller. I found out through the Black grapevine that as the chair of the English Department, he was totally opposed to the notion of Black literature.

For the first time, I was receiving "Cs" on my essays. I'd go to office hours to find out why, and he wouldn't even talk to me. He'd sit behind his desk and with an arrogant smile on his face. His only comment on my papers was "This is not the work befitting a graduate student."

I was only 21 years old and had not encountered this evil from any of my professors before this. He's dead now, but it's something you don't forget. Most of my professors were super cool, very supportive, especially Professor Robert Stallman and Professor Herbert Scott. They encouraged me as a developing scholar and poet. They included Black writers in their American Literature courses, and encouraged my interests to pursue it. Subsequently, I found out that Stallman had been a "beat poet." They created poetry and were also very socially progressive.

Actually, the pushback I got from Mueller was countered by a suggestion from another professor that I should seek publication for an essay I had written on Chester Himes' novel, *Blind Man with a Pistol*. One of my sorority sisters, Hazel Carlos, said she would send it to her cousin, who was an editor at *Ebony* magazine. Her cousin read it, and he passed it on to Hoyt Fuller, who just so happened to be working on a special issue about Chester Himes. Hoyt Fuller contacted me, and it was right on time, because Mueller could not fail a published graduate student.

Well, Hoyt Fuller, who was a graduate of Wayne State University and was a fellow student of Dudley Randall, gave me my first publication, which became the basis of my master's thesis. Subsequently, he published many of my essays and my poetry. I've been publishing consistently, ever since.

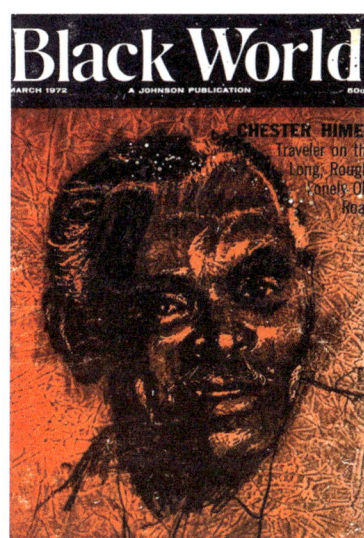

Hoyt W. Fuller was a preeminent literary critic and editor of several black intellectual publications including Black World, which like Ebony was put out by Johnson Publications. March 1972 issue of Black World shown left.

A lot of folks don't know it, but I almost went to law school. I thought I wanted to work in civil rights law, that kind of stuff. I was taking a class to prepare for the LSAT. About a month into the class, I said, I don't want to become a lawyer because it means that this is the kind of literature I'll have to read for the rest of my life. So, even though I'd paid for it and everything, I stopped. You know, there are all of these alternate realities and possibilities, but if I'd done one thing different I probably wouldn't have had the benefit of meeting and being influenced by Dudley Randall.

I had been reading his books. I even did an independent study on Black poetry because you could get all of the Broadside Press books in the bookstore and even the library at Western. Right after I finished my master's at Western, Dudley hired me.

All of this comes together as I'm studying poetry, even quietly aspiring, but I'm really not thinking that I'm good enough to be a poet. I held poetry in such reverence; I figured I could write about poetry and then, in that way, be promoting the literature. Then, when I started working for Dudley it was really a front row seat. It essentially put me in the middle of the Black Arts Movement, which jumped off in 1965. I came into it in 1972, and through Dudley and Broadside I started meeting all of these people and then he asked me if I wrote poetry. I said, well, I try. I never thought when I showed him, he would publish me. But he did, and as part of the famous Broadside series too.

The Book of Melba

Sound Story No. 5
Melba recalls her life-changing encounter with her mentor Dudley Randall, the trailblazing founder of Detroit's Broadside Press.

When you consider the timing, it was a blessing in disguise. The expansion of Black literature as a genre, and the rapid growth of poetry publishing during that time were occurring in Detroit. New York was still the center of mainstream publishing, and a few, select writers were making it into print with those houses. Most of the Black poetry presses at that time would maybe put out one or two books a year. Dudley Randall's Broadside Press started out with a four-books-per-year plan, but by the time I became his assistant editor, he was releasing ten to twelve books a year; it was definitely a production line. He published 90 titles in less than 10 years, with over 500,000 books in multiple printings.

One of the reasons Dudley Randall was the most successful was because he was a poet and a librarian, which meant he knew all poets and any poetry that had been published in the English language. He was also fluent in Russian and German. He also knew how books should look, how they should be printed and bound, so Broadside books were attractive and professional. They were carefully edited and not made with a mimeograph machine. Randall also knew how to network the libraries, where and when to send press releases when the books were published. Hoyt Fuller listed the books in *Black World* magazine. Detroit was a working class town with access to talented printers. Black bookstores had also started opening up in the major cities across the country, and they were ordering his books. One of my responsibilities was to write a press release when a new book came out.

Dudley was also a genius about connecting poetry to the stage. He was the first one to push me out there. In fact, my first reading was with him and Naomi Long Madgett at the Highland Park Library. They were invited to read together, and he introduced me and said, I'm going to give some of my time to Melba so you can hear her poetry. What I remember most about that day is, afterwards Naomi told me how much she liked my work. I still call them "my poetry parents."

Dudley appointed me as his official biographer and he put that in his will. I think that was a really, really smart thing to do, not because it was me, but because he took care of his legacy. I've seen too many poets, artists and entertainers whose estates are just a total mess after they're gone. I was hugely flattered, but to a large extent, intimidated by the responsibility; the preservation of a significant part of the Black artistic heritage of the city of Detroit. It's a tradition that's firmly rooted in change and progress. We see it in the writing, in the art, the music, the creativity. It's always been rooted in challenging the oppression of working people,

A copy of 'Wrestling with the Muse" on display at Melba's home in Detroit.

smashing the whole idea of race and class. These lies about humanity have been imposed on us, reeking hatred and justifying injustice! Having Dudley as my mentor, someone who was part of the Labor Movement in the '30s and the Civil Rights Movement of the '50s and '60s, taught me about commitment and carrying the torch forward.

Sound Story No. 6
Melba pays a visit to one of her favorite public artworks in Detroit.

I've traveled over much of the world. While living and visiting foreign places, I find myself comparing them to home. And when I reflect on this, I am able to see Detroit within a much bigger context and in relationship to the planet. Things happened in Detroit. Major movements. When I went to Bremen, Germany, as a Fulbright Scholar, I immediately bonded with many people there because of their struggle for freedom since the Middle Ages. I didn't know much about its radical history until I arrived there, but I realized parallels with Detroit, as well as the social and cultural movements of the 1960s.

Bremen was founded in the Middle Ages as a free city state. It was a trade city on the Weser, a river, which runs to the North Sea, which reminded me of the Detroit River and the Great Lakes. When Germany became a country in 1848, Bremen literally fought a war to remain independent. Later, Hitler had to send the army to occupy Bremen because when he was elected the citizens voted to secede from Germany. They were like, f--- your Third Reich. Oh man, the history is so intriguing, and such a significant part of its cultural identity, like Detroit. The Bremen connection is still important to me. I was only there for a year, but I keep returning because of the people and the culture.

You don't really think about this legacy stuff until you have to, though I've been dropping bread crumbs along the way in different essays. I suppose I've got to really sit down and finally start my memoirs. It's a joke with my family, but I do see myself retiring from academia. I've also got a lot of ideas in the wings waiting for me. I have a screenplay about Frances Harper. I really would like to see that come to fruition. But I don't know that industry, and you have to have connections. I need to find someone who can help me navigate that terrain.

Once I have more time, I'll probably just go to the cabin in Canada to start figuring things out. I've done so much of my writing up there because when we're on the Georgian Bay, there is no fear, no constant consideration of all of those problematic issues of being Black in America. It's a gift to be with nature like that.

The biggest thing for me personally, is the hope that the poetry, you know, will live on and people will find some value in it regardless of what age you come to it.

I think that's the way most poets and artists feel. But my other theory, though, is that we'll never know until we die, and we may not know s--- when we die. We may just be dead.

Melba's portrait is featured alongside Dudley Randall (far left) and Naomi Long Madgett as part of Detroit artist Nicole Macdonald's Detroit-based poets and publishers series. The mural is located on Trumbull Avenue next to Wayne State University's athletic fields.

The Book of Melba

74

ABOVE Melba in conversation with Michigan Poet Laureate Nandi Comer and others at a reading at Wayne State University in Detroit.

BELOW Melba speaks with museum visitors at the Charles H. Wright Museum of African American History.

1. Conant Gardens is an historic northeast Detroit neighborhood bounded by Nevada and Conant streets, and Seven Mile and Ryan roads. Shubael Conant, an abolitionist and the founder and first president of the Detroit Anti-Slavery Society, was the land's original owner. In the 1920s, scores of Black middle class families bought and in some cases built homes in certain neighborhoods due to a lack of deed restrictions against Black ownership.

2. Robert Hayden, a Detroit native, was the first Black writer to be appointed Consultant in Poetry to the Library of Congress, a role more widely known today as US Poet Laureate. Hayden served from 1976 to 1978.

3. There are 107 colleges or universities identified by the U.S. Department of Education as Historically Black Colleges and Universities (HBCUs). The designation is a result of the HIgher Education Act of 1965.

4. Hoyt W. Fuller was a preeminent literary critic and editor of several black intellectual publications including Black World, which like Ebony was put out by Johnson Publications.

5. Chester Himes was an African American writer celebrated for fiction, autobiographical works and a series of Harlem detective novels.

6. The Black Arts Movement was a Black nationalist movement (1965–1975) focused on music, literature, drama, and the visual arts by Black artists and intellectuals.

7. Naomi Long Madgett was an American poet and publisher. Originally a teacher, she later found fame with her award-winning poems and was also the founder and senior editor of Lotus Press, established in 1972.

8. Bremen is the largest port city on Germany's North Sea coast. It lost its autonomy under the Hitler regime.

9. During World War II, the Battle of Bremen was one of the last battles during the Allied conquest of Germany.

Outro

The Book of Melba

Melba's Garden

Poems

1965

(dedicated to all my Brothers
and Sisters of southwest Detroit,
who did and did not survive)

"Jerry Johnson! Haven't seen you since '65."
    quick flashes
        of friday nights...
    basketball, 99c wine,
    motown jams, and partyin' strong.

"Yeah, haven't seen you since '65."
    '65, when we were all
    talking jive, laughing loud,
    learning little, and losing all.

 when all that mattered was
    the game —"the Big House"
    where Black boys bought manhood
    through short lived fame...
    found on the page of the
            Free Press...
"In Print, Man," they would say
And we would beam about always beating the white boys.

"Whatever happened to...
    he dead too?"
    wine, war, scag, whatever
    for only one superstar rode a basketball
    out of our ford factory fate.
the rest, "in print" in the o-bitch-uary.
But in '65 our world was
    basketball, 99c wine
    and talking jive to the motown sound
not knowing that our friday nights were
    sponsored by ford
as our heroes dribbled themselves
        to death.

The Book of Melba

We Want our City Back

We want our city back.
We want our streetlights on.
We want our garbage gone.
We want our children
playing on playgrounds,
but not with loaded guns.
We want to retire
by the river
and raise collard greens
in abandoned fields.
We want our ancestors
to rest in peace.
We want our city back.

We don't want law and order.
We want justice and jobs.
We don't want small business.
We mean serious business.
No more Mom and Pop wig shops.
No more Mickey D's
rappin' with the homies.
No more Dixie Colonels
serving Kente cloth cuisine.
No more taco supreme.
No more indigestion or
quick-fix politics.
We want our city back.

We don't want police
harassing the homeless
for being without a lease.
We don't want video cops
busting crackheads
with flashlights at night.
We want peacekeepers
to capture real dope men
reclining in respectable privilege.
We want our taxes to track
down real assassins.
We want our city back.

We don't want Euro-centric
or Afro-eccentric edu-macations.
We want a freedom curriculum.
We want a liberated vision
in history remembered.
We don't want our children
crunched like computer chips
to fit in the old world order,
worshiping slave holding
societies in Egypt and Greece.
We want the board of education
to take a lie detector test
for neglect of the intellect,
for assault on our children's senses.
We don't want them to be GM execs,
or rejects in labor camps.
We want dignity,
not cupidity.
We want our city back.

We want the river dragged
for distraught souls.
We want our homes rebuilt.
We want the guilty
to pay a greed tax
for the living they stole.
We want our city back.

Hey! We ain't going away
like fugitives escaping
to Canaday!
Our backs are up
against the wall.
This is our clarion call.
Feed the hungry.
Clothe the ragged.
Heal the sick.
Enlighten the ignorant.
Punish the wicked.
And raise the dead!

We want our street lights on.
We want our garbage gone.
We want to be rid
of smack and crack.
We want to retire
by the river.
We want our ancestors
to rest is peace.
We are claiming our history
seizing the hour.
Cause, we mean to take
our city back.

yari yari: writing for the future

my father did not rape me.
my mother does not hate me.
and I'm at peace with my god.
but, i write to stop the pain.

i write to clean the rain.
i write to incite ocean waves.
i communicate with
the eyes of tornadoes,
and sift through the ash
of volcanoes.
i tell trees to reclaim
their rightful terrain.
i write to stop the pain.

i write apologies to blind fish
swimming with injured fins.
i send get well cards
to crippled, three-legged frogs
who want to hop again.
i write editorials to applaud
dolphins who inspired
an environmental conference.
I write prayers for the noble elk
slain, beheaded and displayed.
i write to stop the pain.

i write pleas for human beings.
i write so white folks
can take off their skin.
i write for black teens
pulling up baggy jeans,
singing syncopated rhythms
in discordant rhyme schemes.
i write for young women
with spiraling, sculptured hair,
reaching for pastel sunsets
painted on false fingernails
i write to stop the pain.

i speak in tongues and
swear in ancient languages
i encode with signs and
transcribe tragic images
i write as a reason to be
i write poetry that bleeds
i write to stop the pain.

this museum was once a dream

Dedication poem for the Charles H. Wright Museum of African American History

this museum
was once a dream
inscribed inside
the walls of
slave quarters
the gates were guarded
by ghosts in colored bottles
of glass swinging from string
between bleeding trees
they held secrets
of millions severed
from their
stories.

brick by brick
memories rebuilt
the amber flare
of ancient
Abyssinian splendor.
the ancestors insisted
like the swelling
of the mighty Mississippi
like escaping fugitives
tracing moss from
limb to limb,
from Alabama
through Tennessee,
from Africa through
Tuskegee.

swollen fingers molded
like mortar along
the angles of pyramids
following lost rivers
and vanishing borders
recollecting cotton blossoms
strewn beside a
narrow stream
of blue light
splitting the distance

the entrance
to this museum
was hidden within
memories rediscovered.
the dream restored
on the frozen path
of freedom
was the imprint of
God's great reach
and the immortal
human story

The Book of Melba

burial of a building

upon the 1998 implosion of the J.L. Hudson's department store in Detroit

when they bring
a building down,
when they make
history absent,
when they implode
a cistern of memories
into a basement grave,
where do the
ghosts go?

are they given
an eviction notice?
do they read
the headlines
of runaway newspapers
rumbling down
the street?
or do they
pass on
a posting
caught on a
jagged nail or
transfixed to
crumbling concrete?

did the ghost
of the "light-skinned
colored girl"
who ran elevator
number 5
call a meeting
between floors
to discuss
the demise?
or did the last
of the charmed,
posed mannequins
hiding in the
bridal suite
of dressing rooms,
send out the
fatal alarm?

perhaps, one of the
under-employed,
excavating the remains
for bronze fixtures and
copper veins,
left an echo
so disturbing
it alerted
returning spirits —
disrupted their
eternal shopping
for imported,
after dinner mints,
for that exquisite dress
with the perfect fit,
for that pin-striped suit
for the anniversary
occasion, or for
another matching set
of muffs and scarves
for Xmas past
celebrations.

did the ghosts follow
our footprints
to sit atop our houses?
or did they hover
next to high rise towers
and likewise, point
translucent fingers
and clink champagne glasses
filled with misty laughter?
or did the blast
call their skeletons
to attention,
disrupt such earth
bound musings
and with the wind
scatter them
with dust, ashes
and disoriented pigeons?

another landmark gone—
another space left behind,
another hole in a story,
another burial
to collect bones,
another place
from where ghosts
are gone.

A Mingus Among Us and a Walden Within Us

for Donald Walden (1938–2008)

Dexter Gordon
glanced back,
saw Donald Walden
taking Giant Steps.

So, Dexter held the gate,
makin' the jazz greats wait—
Monk, Bird, Coltrane
the contentious Miles
the tumultuous Lateef
and the sultry Billie —
makin' a wake
for the sax man
from Detroit
by way of
St. Louie,
representin' bebop
breaking fixed notes,
traversing linear scales,
and all repressive
constrictions impaled
on the music sheets,
resisting the
inconvenience
of mortal skin
when spirit enchants
song and rules of
Earth bound
dominions
diminish.

In the "D"
he was called
"the bebop police,"
who styled in
razor sharp
GQ slacks
as distinctive
as his tenor sax,
articulating
transformative
sets marking
planets.

Yeah,
there is a
Mingus
among us
but there is
a Donald Walden
within us.

Blow Marcus Blow

for Marcus Belgrave (1936–2015) *

There's jazz around the corner / just beyond the gold gate, / Hallelujah jazz.
—Art Paul Schlosser

Marcus blows away
Our Detroit blues,
I said,
Marcus Belgrave
blows away our
never-ending blues
he breaks off
circuitous sounds
inside the city's
contentious womb.

Motown lyrics swing,
as bebop registers
iconic scales
that make
spirits roar
even when

Winter comes
and locks
in the cold.

we shiver with
uncertainty within
shifting winds—
this end of an era
we mourn with the
passing of a true
Renaissance man,
and then celebrate
his reunion with
Dizzy, Miles
and Satchmo
kicking it with
Cox,
McKinney
and Walden
inside timelessness —
the freedom zone
of eternal jazz.

So, blow Gabriel.
Go blow your horn
Cause jazz is
Round the corner,
"Hallelujah jazz,"
and Marcus Belgrave
is joinin' your band
in the Promise Land.

Blow Marcus Blow!
Blow Marcus Blow!

*Marcus Belgrave (1936–2015) was the 2009 Kresge Eminent Artist

The Bass Is Woman

for Marion Hayden*

At a left – angled tilt, adjacent to

her throat
Marion mind
melds with this
magnificent
instrument.

Lithe, swift
fingers
restringing

eighth notes
in cut time
against
bare-knuckle
restraints
releasing stress
from neck
past breasts
through a
navel leading
into a womb
gifting violet
riffs like sweet
rose water
brimming inside
uninhibited
thick hips
that swing
and sway,
dancing on
ripples of
unreachable
prayers.

Her brown
curves ground
earth tones
at the base
of rhythm—
the back-
bone of song.

The bass
is woman.

*Marion Hayden was a 2016 Kresge Artist Fellow

the rose in the garden

For Rosemarie Luvall

we did not grow
between concrete
cracks like weeds in
an asphalt jungle.
we were planted
by parents
in discrete cottages
underneath protective
tree branches in
a mythical garden.

like her name,
she was a rose
delicate and tender
with a voice
as sweet as
the lilt of a child's.
she nurtured
kindness as intelligence,
trimmed jagged
edges with literature,
and groomed us
into refined,
complex citizens
sent to challenge
a city waiting
to trap us in
classic betrayal
or to cast us
into riddles
crueler than the
confluence of our
own errors.

even when we
wept in the dark,
she never locked
the gate
or turned out
the light
above the
kitchen
window.

the death of a time

you receive
these letters
on a curl
of smoke
rising from
your cigar.
it is the
earliest moment
of morning
when light
is a quiet pink
stretched across
the reflection between
the Detroit River
and the Canadian clouds.

i write you
reluctantly,
because I have
few words of
encouragement
only faith
and an ongoing
devotion for
a world
we keep
in the deepest
focus of
our dreams.

when you peer
through these words
i pray they
will not dissuade
your belief in us Ché.
for it is not
the retreat
or the disparity
of our numbers
that concerns me,
but rather
the madness
that passes for
militancy in these
lost years.

blackness used
to be a declaration
of defiance,
of self defense.
now,
Africa in America
is a desire
for respectability,
a dance with republican
governors on
inaugural ballroom floors—
overtures that muffle
a numbness
more frightening
than the burgeoning
fascism and the
inaction accompanying
the craving for money
and the quest
for acceptance.

identity is a
departure from the land,
a retrenchment of
our indigenous ancestry,
a narrowness that inhibits
memory breathing
in the Americas,
thought molded without
clay or stone.
and in these
empty air pockets
our children are
born like filters
where innocence
has no value
or bearing
on the future,
where everything
is a corporation
or a government
and they police
our poetry
and jail
our imaginations
banished to the
middle of the corn fields
to mourn
the death of a time,
while the reaper
ravages those still
wandering the cities.

we could not
shout loud enough
to discompose them,
to disconcert their
ears sewn shut,
or their eyes
crusted closed.
they did not want
to find the lamps
aligning history
or the difficult path
leading us
to the disturbance.

maybe, this is
an end point,
where we ascend
with the decline
of butterflies,
where we disembody
after a respite
in the cocoon.

C'est Une Histoire Extraordinaire

for Michele and Genieve Fabre

We escape
to *Paris*
to liberate
the American
dictionary,
to write
ourselves out
of metaphors
cursing the color
of expatriate
authors estranged
from our native
tongue.

And you are
ambassadors
on journeys
to foreign
literature,
harboring
inscriptions
of black aesthctics
condemned for
angry cadence
yearning to speak
as freely as bebop
transcending grief
making love
by *le Seine*
when the Spring
of `68
merged centuries
of revolutions
convening with
Negritude to
celebrate Josephine's
magnificent derriere
and Ellington's
luminous suites.

You contradict
snide dismissals
of Wright's Bigger,
you explicate
reasoning for
violent imagery
distilled into
poetic beauty
and theorize
that masking
is coded magic
in plays like
Sidney Bechet's
vertical schematics
romancing your
affection into
marriage,
while you reveal
mystery within
our subversive
imaginary of
nouveau noire
protest art.

We escape
to *Paris,*
and you are
our embassy.
*c'est une histoire
extraordinaire.*

2001

It is science fiction.

most citizens
oscillate
between
obscurity
and insignificance,
giving and scraping
the walls
of the tomb.

their signatures
cringing there,
confused
and ordinary.

the accumulation
of pain and
the ambiguity
of guilt
can no longer
be forgotten
in withered weekends
by the fireplace
with dry wine
an another
mistaken identity,
ignorant of
the humiliation
of the phone
screaming
at 3 a.m.
about a bullet
in a chest
and a wife
with a knife.

Believe
what we feel.

too much death
is buried
between
our eyes
to listen
to the limits
of the living.

We are the unknown,
invisible Indians
planting corn.
meridians
who walk
in sidewalk seams,
spinning the spiral
in between,
blending clouds
above
midnight trees.

waiting...
for fresh breath
of Mayans
spreading tears
on the dawn.

somebody stole your tennis shoes

It's 1984
and they're knocking
at your door.
WAKE UP!
Your house
Is on fire,
Your lover is a liar,
And somebody stole
Your shoes.

He was hanging
Off the chair,
Then sitting on the sink,
Waiting by the mailbox
Smoking cigarettes.

Quick!

You got
15 seconds left

To scrap this
TV script.

Don't smile
at plastic flowers
or wish for a
black Corvette,
or believe imitation cheese
grows on supermarket shelves.
while drinking bottled water,
they painted your fingernails,
while staring at the TV set,
they clipped your ears,
parted your brain,
and told you
eternal bliss
is endless,
mindless
sex.
It's 1984,
And they're knocking
At your door.
Your house
Is on fire,
Your lover
is a liar and
they're sending you
to a polluted garden.

WAKE UP!
Somebody stole
Your orange & purple,
Psychedelic,
Made in Taiwan,
High top,
Tennis shoes.

Bremen, December 19, 1983
Detroit, Feb. 2006

The Book of Melba

Melba's Garden

Essays

Beyond her career as a poet, Melba Joyce Boyd is also a prolific essayist and biographer. Known for making blunt arguments about key cultural moments and historic figures, she has published writings in more than 100 literary and scholarly journals.

The Black Arts Movement (1965–1977) was an outgrowth of the Civil Rights Movement, and the impetus of this cultural revolution was the consequence of an artist/activist consciousness that embraced the notion of race pride, self determination and the need to engage in institution building. In the Midwest, Chicago and Detroit were key cities during this era because they contained large and industrious African American populations and housed major cultural institutions. The Du Sable Museum of African American History and Art, The Kuumba Workshop, the Organization of Black Art and Culture and The Negro Digest operated in Chicago; while the Broadside Press, Rappa House, Concept East and the Shrine of the Black Madonna were the loci of much activity in Detroit. Sustained through collective interests and burgeoning activities, interaction between the two cultural communities was largely the result of proximity and personal histories.

The Black Arts Movement is usually associated with those artists whose careers became most visible. The younger writers, such as LeRoi Jones (Imamu Baraka), Don L. Lee (Haki Madhubuti) and Nikki Giovanni are often the focus of discussion and their militant styles delineate what is regarded as characteristic of the literature. However, no era stands independent of previous time periods. Even though the vocabulary of the Black Arts Movement was influenced by the Black Liberation Movement, the leadership responsible for the institutions that provided the forums for literary militancy stood on the shoulders of writers whose expertise and experience were grounded in the preceding decades.

For some undetermined reason, prominent cultural leaders were often poets. Perhaps, as prophets and visionaries they were particularly suited for the role of institutional directors. At any rate, women poets were as critical to the era as their male counterparts and counterpoints. The poetry of Gwendolyn Brooks, Margaret Walker, Margaret Danner, who died in 1984, and to a lesser extent, Margaret Burroughs, greatly influenced the aesthetic development of the younger poets. Although these women writers embraced the goal of African American freedom and their aesthetic expressions articulated race pride in imagery configured to counter the inhumane stereotypes of black people, there was also a class consciousness that permeated their poetry because their historical development during the Great Depression (1930s) and the Labor Movement (1930–40s) encouraged a deeper understanding of the economics of discrimination.

All of these women poets at one time or another lived in Chicago, and for a very brief period, Margaret Danner lived in Detroit; however, they all frequented Detroit throughout their careers. Their poetry was published by Broadside Press during the late 1960s and early 1970s, and they gave readings to enthusiastic crowds in Detroit and Chicago during the Black Arts Movement. But in as much as a romantic recollection would be more satisfactory for the reconstruction of a noble history, a closer examination of relationships revealed the differences and difficulties within the camp. The politics of personalities sometimes strained friendships and created conflicts. Hence, it was a challenging and colorful period when the pretense of race solidarity was the reigning rhetoric, but not necessarily the practice.

From: "Prophets for a New Day": The Cultural Activism of Margaret Danner, Margaret Burroughs, Gwendolyn Brooks and Margaret Walker During the Black Arts Movement, Wayne State University.

One afternoon when my car was in the shop and Dudley drove me home so I would not have to wait on the bus, we talked about writing, American literature, racial discrimination — a collage of topics. When he asked me, "What do you think about whites teaching Black literature?" I paused because I suspected he was trying to figure out my cultural politics. I told him, "I went to university when the subject wasn't even offered until we, the students, protested and demonstrated to get courses in Black studies. There wasn't a single Black professor in the English department, and if it hadn't been for Professor Murphy, a white man who studied Black literature on his own, the course wouldn't have happened, at least not while I was a student. I'd been reading Black literature on my own, but when he offered to teach the course, I got the chance to study it in the classroom as an English major, and I was thankful for the opportunity.

"I agree, but you know a lot of Blacks don't feel that way," Dudley said quietly.

"I know, but I also wanted to know how the literature worked, and that meant more than just talking about the problem of racism. I wanted to figure out how the words worked, which most of the Black students in the class weren't interested in. They took the course because they mistakenly thought it would be easy, and the lectures on symbolism, metaphors, literary style and vocabulary were not that interesting to them."

A few weeks later, Dudley asked me, "Do you write poetry?" I admitted that I did, but I said it reluctantly because I kept my poems in notebooks, only to be read by the uncritical eyes of family and close friends. My poetry professor, Robert Stillman, at Western Michigan University encouraged me to write poetry, but as a student of literature, I held poetry in such reverence that I never thought that I could ever publish any of my own. But I was complimented by Dudley's inquiry and both curious and anxious to get his appraisal. I showed him the poem "1965," and he made one comment about developing parallelism to enhance its form. I realized at once that the key to his editorial judgment was that he could read a poem and determine how to strengthen it without infringing on its originality or thematic intentions.

After I reworked the poem and showed it to him, he said, "I'm going to publish this in the Broadside Series." I shared more poems with him, and he further encouraged me by inviting me to read poetry with him and Naomi Long Madgett at the Highland Park Public Library.

From: *Wrestling with the Muse: Dudley Randall and the Broadside Press*, Melba Joyce Boyd , 2003.

Detroit poets cling to the craziness of resistance in the face of literary traditions, and they scoff at the rules of conventional politics. Despite the conservative shift of society, Detroit poets are melded and embellished by diversity. They delve into the unknown depths and garner creative energy as ideology.

The poets of this time and place recover the dead streets of a once vital Paradise Valley. They remember and give voice to ghosts living underneath newly paved streets, deadened by hollow corridors and dreams deprived of passion. From the vanquished magic of Spanish accents that linger in the aftermath of confrontations with American English, poets save and savor the grace of ancient, indigenous sensibility. From the unseen strength of Slavic undertones, poets inhabit corners of vigilant neighborhoods. Contesting the onslaught of natural and unnatural storms, they invent new visions and open an old life to an earth renewed.

Detroit poets write about the city as a living entity. … These poets listen to the hum of history and the clash of metal. They reveal life still striving in the refuge civilization forgets, but never forgives. … They write under the shade of weathered trees, bathe their words in a river that withstands the undertow of the Great Lakes, and with each new poem rebuild meaning for the city.

From : *Abandoned Automobile, Detroit City Poetry* 2001, Edited by Melba Joyce Boyd and M.L. Liebler.

The subterfuge of America's sexual psyche is so deep-seated that women who have been victimized are victims even before the assault.

The woman is not to be believed at any cost, especially the Black woman, whose sexual legacy in this country has been the Jezebel — the loose woman, who instigates her own rape. The periphery of comments made by many women and men, even when they believed Anita Hill was harassed, is reflexive of a cultural code that dictates: "As a Black woman, she should have checked him and got him straight from the get-go, but she should have never exposed him in front of white America." In addition to being accorded so little respect and consideration, Black women are still expected to eradicate the onslaught of male madness and to endure indignities simply because to reveal the truth about the devils in the camp would be an embarrassment for the "race." Conversely, if Black Americans exhibited stronger political and moral positions on such issues, we would not continue to be consumed by the deluge of contradictions that, historically, have blamed the victim instead of the perpetrator. And in our case, what could be more evident than the fact that slavery is still used by bigots as a reference to demean and degrade us instead of American democracy.

Why is it that women are denied full humanity and must shoulder the weight of everybody else's weaknesses, especially when the character in question is perfectly prepared to sell us, and even his own mother and sister, down the river in order to achieve fame and prestige by cavorting with the anti-Civil Rights president and his New World Order?

The incapacity of human beings to evolve beyond the superficial, beyond the arbitrary categories of race (which, in our case, were contrived by the slaveholding class to perpetuate our enslavement and subsequent second-class citizenship) and deal with the truth is directly related to the confusion and conflict revealed in responses to the Thomas-Hill hearings. The stratification of race, gender, and class can no longer be assessed by token representation. The New World Order is the Old World Order constructed to the benefit of global corporations. Representation in the hierarchy by people of color, women, even homosexuals, too often reflects a careful selection of well trained, articulate functionaries who facilitate the expectations and directives of that ruling order.

From: Collard Greens, Clarence Thomas, and the High-Tech Rape of Anita Hill, *Court of Appeal, The Black Community Speaks Out on the Racism and Sexual Politics of Thomas vs. Hill , 1992,* Edited By The Black Scholar.

I knew my brother John was intensely involved with a group of frustrated young men angered by the havoc, death, and destruction that the heroin dope trade caused in Black communities throughout Detroit. I thought the meetings he attended were like many gatherings, infused with youthful zeal and enthusiastic political rhetoric. What I did not know was that these meetings were strategic, and that he was part of an underground cadre that harassed and threatened dope dealers until they shut down their predatory businesses and moved out of neighborhoods. This inevitably led to a clash with an undercover Stop Robberies Enjoy Safe Streets (STRESS) unit.

On the night of December 4, 1972, three young Black men retaliated when a STRESS unit blasted a hole in the rear window of their Volkswagen. All four policemen were seriously wounded. A second shootout on December 27 left one officer dead and a second one critically injured. The three men involved in the shootouts were John Percy Boyd Jr. (my brother), Hayward Brown (my first cousin), and Mark Bethune. In retaliation, the Detroit Police Department lashed out at the Black community and targeted the families and friends of Boyd, Brown, and Bethune. The evening following the first shootout, a battalion of police (at least twenty) broke down the front door of my parents' house with a battering ram and held me, my mother, my stepbrother, and my two-year-old baby brother at gunpoint.

As they ransacked the house, I tried to calm my screaming baby brother and a nervous policeman with a carbine rifle aimed at us yelling, "Freeze! Or I'll shoot!" In a direct and deliberate tone, I kept repeating, "Can't you see, I'm holding a baby? Can't you see, I'm holding a baby?"

I was ordered to sit on the sofa in the living room next to my mother, but I became so angry I defied them and followed the police, who were ransacking our home. I don't anger easily, and in lieu of the circumstances, I even surprised myself as I began to challenge the police, demanding that they produce a search warrant — swearing at them, and reprimanding them for violating our constitutional rights. To wit, they seemed surprised and annoyed, because I refused to stop my rant despite their threatening weapons.

From: *In Hot Pursuit: The Deadly Consequences of Detroit Police Oppression* published in The Journal of Law in Society.

PRELUDE

> If all the wealthy and influential honored were men as the Bible teaches, would they ever throw their lives between God's sunshine and the shivering poor, and fence in leagues of land by bonds and chains and title deeds, when land and water and air and light are God's own gifts and heritage to man? Should they not remember that the humblest and poorest human being who enters the threshold of life comes as the child of a King, and at the feast of life be received as the guest of a living God? Would not the vision of Christian grow clearer to see, beneath the darkened skin and shaded countenance, poverty of condition, or the dust and grime of labor, the human soul all written over with the hand marks of Divinity, and the common chains of humanity?

Frances Ellen Watkins Harper,
Philadelphia, 1898

Like the crocuses, we awaken every spring, the sun still calling our color, the rain refilling the rivers. The Afro-American spiral of history has no clear opening or closing. It should not be flattened by innocuous memory or inflated by postured revisions. Superimposing the resiliency of Frances Harper's path, I encountered the ongoing conflicts of human despair and defiant resistance. The shouting sidewalks tell us what is too obvious — we are running out of time. The people fill their shrinking space with blasting music. Their faces, hung-heavy, lifted by liquor and the death crack of cocaine, contour a known fact nearly nobody notices. The quagmire of hopelessness steals more grandchildren in a week than Harriet "Moses" Tubman ever delivered. This retrieval of Harper's inscription is a resonance of resistance, confronting the cryptic irony of human history.

Melba Joyce Boyd,
Detroit, 1994

From: *Discarded Legacy Politics and Poetics in the Life of Frances E. W. Harper* (1825–1911).

My interest in poetry occurred just prior to my entry into American activism on April 4, 1968, when Dr. Martin Luther King, Jr. was assassinated. It was two days after my eighteenth birthday. I joined a student protest at Western Michigan University to acknowledge the tragedy of King's death and illuminate American hypocrisy. While occupying the Student Union Building, the Michigan National Guard threatened to forcibly remove us. Fortunately, the Board of Regents of the University intervened and accommodated our demands for a Center for Black Studies and the establishment of a Martin Luther King Scholarship Fund for students of color.

[Gil] Scott-Heron's poetry inspired my aspirations to become a poet, and his cultural presence informed my poetics and my politics, which was still the case during a historical moment in Germany. In the spring of 1984, Gil Scott-Heron appeared in concert at the University of Bremen in West Germany. The audience was largely peace protesters who identified themselves as " '68ers," a term rooted in European activism that developed in tandem with the Civil Rights and Peace Movements in the United States. At the time, I was a Fulbright professor, teaching American literature, protesting the war, and writing poetry. And, like Gil Scott-Heron, I was collaborating with a jazz musician, Michael Sievert, for performances.

> Green poems are written
> In blue violet striping amber.
> Skeletons signature
> The sidewalks of Bremen:
>> "Wir waren dafür.
>> Jetzt sind wir tot.
>> Was wird der nächste
>> Krieg bringen?"[i]

Shortly after I arrived in Germany in the summer of 1983, I attended a concert featuring Mitch Ryder and the Detroit Wheels in Frankfurt. The venue was overflowing, and people went wild when Mitch Ryder announced: "Ich bin aus Amerika, aber er ist nicht mein Präsident," ("I am from America, but he is not my President.") This public dismissal of Reagan was a declaration of the band's political stance against what was happening in Germany. Mitch Ryder was voicing the anti-war sentiments of our generation in the U.S. and connecting with a cross-continental peace movement that was vital and thriving in this historical context. I was invigorated and excited that members of this rock 'n' roll band from Detroit contained members who had attended Pershing High School, which was also my alma mater. Another irony was that the short-range, nuclear missiles were called Pershing II's, a reference in my poem, "Intro: the fourteenth flamingo."[ii]

> Wie ein amerikanisches Drama,
> with black and brown
> Soldiers drinking coca cola
> escorting General Black
> Jack Pershing
> reincarnated as a Missile
> through the Black Forest
> under "saurer Regen"
> to wait for Rotkäppchen
> mit Kermit Kohl.

Like Mitch Ryder and the Detroit Wheels, the same radical sentiments of the 1960s–70s ushered Gil Scott-Heron's political discourse and poetics onto the global stage. The momentum continued, and progressive popular music was still relevant in the 1980s during the Cold War. In particular, the face-off on the border between East and West Germany persisted, and the United States deployed Pershing II Missiles while the Soviet Union matched the threat with similar weapons of nuclear destruction. My poem, "Wingless Spiders,"[iii] is a description of this duel in a country that had no political power to stop this threat by the two world powers occupying and controlling their divided space:

> The Left gun
> and the Right gum
> face the Line.
> Tanks wait
> by train tracks
> under the trees.
> Leaves listen
> to throbbing hills
> tell legends
> about men
> with double vision—
> wingless Spiders
> who will sacrifice
> ancient
> and injured
> cities.
>
> I hold hands
> with the women.
> We make a ring
> around the children.
> The men plant
> flowers forever
> to never forget,
> in our throats
> the trigger
> is cocked.

The Book of Melba

Meanwhile, the Anti-War Movement escalated its nonviolent resistance efforts to dissuade the superpowers from igniting their "limited nuclear war"[iv] in Germany.

Scott-Heron's poem, "B Movie" (1981) was very popular with this German audience because it criticizes Ronald Reagan's reactionary, Republican politics in world affairs that advocated an aggressive, pro-nuclear strategy against the Soviet Union. Scott-Heron recounts Reagan's progressive politics during the 1950s when he was president of the Screen Actors Guild and gallantly stood up to Senator Joseph McCarthy's harassment of actors and directors in the movie industry for their liberal politics or affiliations with socialists or communists. But then the song mocks Reagan for abandoning and inverting his activist politics by calling him Rea-gon and metaphorically projecting America's national identity as a "B" movie.

> You go give them liberals hell Ronnie.
> That was the mandate to the new Captain
> Bligh on the new ship of fools
> It was doubtlessly based on his chameleon performance of the past:
> as a Liberal Democrat
> As the head of the Studio Actors Guild, when other celluloid saviors were cringing in terror from McCarthy, Ron stood tall
> It goes all the way back from Hollywood to hillbilly
> From Liberal to libelous, from
> "Bonzo" to Birch idol, born again
> Civil rights, women's rights, gay rights: …it's all wrong
> Call in the cavalry to disrupt this perception of freedom gone wild
> God damn it, first one wants freedom, then the whole damn world wants freedom

"We Almost Lost Detroit" also made an indelible impact on the German audience, anticipating annihilation. A nuclear disaster at a power plant almost occurred, which would have decimated my hometown, killing millions of people. This song is a warning to the world.

> And we almost lost Detroit
> This time
> How will we ever get over
> Losing our minds
>
> Just thirty miles from Detroit
> Lies a giant power station
> It ticks each night as the city sleeps
> Seconds from annihilation
> But no one stopped to think
> about the people or
> How they will survive

From: "Fred Was Feelin' It": Echoes of Frederick Douglass in the Voices of Gil Scott-Heron and Donald Glover/Childish Gambino, 2023, Melba Joyce Boyd.

[i] Translation from German to English:

"Wir waren dafür.   "We were before,
Jetzt sind wir tot.   Yet, now we are dead
Was wird der nächste   What will the next
Krieg bringen?"   War bring?"

[ii] In these lines of the poem, I describe the German experience as an American Drama with the military presence and the threat of nuclear destruction. "General Blackjack Pershing" is a name General Pershing acquired because during World War I, he commanded the Black troops in the segregated U.S. Army, and "sauer Regen" is German for "sour rain," which in English sounds like "sour Reagan." "Rotkäppchen" is Little Red Ridinghood" from the fairy tale, and "Kermit Kohl" refers to Prime Minister Kohl as Reagan's puppet, like Kermit the frog.

[iii] Melba Joyce Boyd, "Wingless Spiders," *Thirteen Frozen Flamingoes* (Bremen, Germany: Die Certel Press, 1984), p. 13.

Bibliography

Melba Joyce Boyd poems
reprinted for this publication

From *Broadside No. 66 Broadside Series*, December 1972, First and only Broadside printing of 500 copies, Broadside Press, Detroit.
    1965 by Melba Joyce Boyd

From *RESPECT | The Poetry of Detroit Music*, Edited by Jim Daniels and M.L. Liebler, Michigan State University Press, Detroit, 2020.
    Blow Marcus Blow
    for Marcus Belgrave (1936–2015)
    A Mingus Among Us and
    a Walden Within Us
    for Donald Walden (1938–2008)
    The Bass Is Woman
    for Marion Hayden

From *Letters to Ché*, Melba Joyce Boyd, Ridgeway Press, Roseville, MI, 1996.
    the death of a time

From *the province of literary cats*, Melba Joyce Boyd, Past Tents Press, Ferndale, MI, 2002.
    this museum was once a dream
    Dedication poem for the
    Charles H. Wright Museum
    yari yari: writing for the future

From *Death Dance of a Butterfly*, Melba Joyce Boyd, Past Tents Press, Ferndale, MI, 2012.
    C'est une Historie Extraordinaire

From *blues music sky of mourning: the German poems*, Melba Joyce Boyd, Past Tents Press, Ferndale, MI 2006.
    somebody stole your tennis shoes

From *The Journal of Law in Society*, Wayne State University Law School, Vol.18, No.2 Fall 2018.
    In Hot Pursuit The Deadly
    Consequences of Detroit Police
    Oppression

From *Discarded Legacy Politics and Poetics in the Life of Frances E. W. Harper (1825–1911)*, Melba J. Boyd, Wayne State University Press, Detroit, 1994.
    Prelude

From *Abandon Automobile, Detroit City Poetry 2001,* Edited by Melba Joyce Boyd and M.L. Liebler, Wayne State University Press, Detroit, 2001.
    Introduction

From *Songs for Maya*, Melba Joyce Boyd, Broadside Press, Detroit, 1982
    2001

Select Works, Citations and Awards

**Dr. Melba Joyce Boyd,
2023 Kresge Eminent Artist**

Distinguished Professor
Wayne State University
Department of African American Studies
College of Liberal Arts and Sciences

Education and Academic Career

EDUCATION

University of Michigan,
Doctor of Arts, English
1979

Western Michigan University
MA, English
1972

Western Michigan University,
Major: English; Minor: Communications,
1971

State of Michigan
Secondary Education Teaching Certificate,
1971

ACADEMIC APPOINTMENT HISTORY

Promoted to WSU Distinguished Professor
2005

Appointed to Department Chair
2005–2016, 1996–2002

Promoted to Full Professor
2001

Appointed to Associate Professor and Awarded Tenure
Wayne State University
1993

Awarded Tenure
University of Michigan
1990

Promoted to Associate Professor
Ohio State University
1988

Appointed to Assistant Professor
University of Iowa
1983

FACULTY APPOINTMENTS AT OTHER INSTITUTIONS

University of Michigan
Center for Afro-American and African Studies
Adjunct Professor, 1992–present

Fudan University
Shanghai, China
Visiting Professor
2009

University of Michigan-Flint
African-American Studies Program
Director and Associate Professor
1989–93, Tenured 1990

Ohio State University
Department of Black Studies and Center for Women's Studies
Associate Professor
1988–89

University of Iowa
Department of English and Black World Studies,
Assistant Professor,
1983–88

Colgate University
Department of English and Black and Latino Studies Program
Visiting Professor
1986

University of Bremen
West Germany
Department of English and American Studies
Senior Fulbright Lecturer
1983–84

University of Iowa
Visiting Professor of Afro-American Literature,
1982–83

Wayne County Community College
Instructor
1972–82

Shaw College of Detroit
Humanities Department
Instructor
1974–76

PROFESSIONAL SOCIETY MEMBERSHIPS

Academy of Scholars
Collegium for African American Research
Association for the Study of African American Life and History
American Studies Association

Awards and Honors

2019
Elected to the Academy of Scholars
Wayne State University

2015
Service Award
Association for the Study of African American Life and History

Service Award
International Institute of Detroit

2013
Michigan Notable Book Award for Poetry,
Death Dance of a Butterfly

2012
Sojourner Truth Meritorious Award
National Association of Negro Business and Professional Women's Association

2010
Independent Publishers Book of the Year,
Gold Award in Poetry,
Roses and Revolutions: The Selected Writings of Dudley Randall

Finalist for ForeWord Book of the Year Award,
Roses and Revolutions: The Selected Writings of Dudley Randall

Finalist for NAACP Image Award in Poetry,
Roses and Revolutions: The Selected Writings of Dudley Randall

Library of Michigan, Top 20 Books on Michigan History and Culture,
Roses and Revolutions: The Selected Writings of Dudley Randall

The Women's Committee Award
Charles H. Wright Museum of African American History

2009
50 Women of Excellence Award
The Michigan Chronicle

2007
Heritage Award
Anthony Wayne Society

2004
Black Caucus Honor Award in Nonfiction,
American Library Association
for *Wrestling with the Muse: Dudley Randall and the Broadside Press*

1996
Award for Outstanding Achievements in the Literary Arts
Frances E. W. Harper Literary Society

1995
Award for Literary Contributions to African American Culture
Links Incorporated, Ann Arbor Chapter

President's Affirmative Action Award
Wayne State University

1991
Faculty Research Grant Award,
University of Michigan
Rackham Graduate College

1990
Recognition for Major Contributions to African American Culture
Society of the Culturally Concerned

1989
Research and Publication Award
Ohio State University, College of the Humanities

1985, 1987, 1988
Old Gold Summer Research Fellowship
The University of Iowa

1981
Individual Artist Award, Poetry,
Michigan Council for the Arts

1978
Literature Award
National Conference of Artists,
Michigan Chapter

Publication Award
National Endowment for the Arts

Poetry

BOOKS AUTHORED

Death Dance of a Butterfly.
Detroit: Past Tents Press, 2013.

blues music sky of mourning: the German poems.
Detroit: Past Tents Press, 2006.

the province of literary cats.
Detroit: Past Tents Press, 2002.

Letters to Ché.
Detroit: Ridgeway Press, 1996.

The Inventory of Black Roses.
Detroit: Past Tents Press, 1989.

Lied fur Maya/Song for Maya.
Osnabruck Bilingual Editions of Minority Authors, West Germany: WURF Verlag Press, 1989.

Thirteen Frozen Flamingoes.
Bremen, West Germany: Die Certel Press, Universitat Bremen, 1984.

Song for Maya.
Detroit: Broadside Press and Detroit River Press, 1983.

Cat Eyes and Dead Wood.
Detroit: Fallen Angel Press, 1978.
Commissioned Work

ALSO PUBLISHED

Poetry in Response to the Art of Romare Bearden: "Mirrored Vision," "Diego and Romare: from a photograph by Frank Stewart," "The Dinner: from a photograph by Frank Stewart," and "Quilting Time," High Museum of Art, Atlanta, Georgia, January 2020.

"Maple Red: a poetic interlude with the painting by Ed Clark," Detroit Institute of Arts, poem installed beneath painting, 2008.

"Phoenix Rising: Mayor Coleman Alexander Young," Coleman A. Young Foundation, 2007.

Lines from "We Want Our City Back," in the sculpture, Transcending: Michigan's Tribute to Labor, installed in downtown Detroit, 2003.

this museum was once a dream, poem for The Charles H. Wright Museum of African American History, Detroit, engraved in bronze on dedication plaque, 1997.

Scholarly Writing

BOOKS AUTHORED

Wrestling with the Muse: Dudley Randall and the Broadside Press. New York: Columbia University Press, 2004.

Discarded Legacy: Politics and Poetics in the Life of Frances E. W. Harper (1825–1911). Detroit: Wayne State University Press, 1994.

BOOKS EDITED

Roses and Revolutions: The Selected Writings of Dudley Randall. Detroit: Wayne State University Press, 2009.

Abandon Automobile: Detroit Poetry 2001. Edited with M. L. Liebler, Detroit: Wayne State University Press, 2001.

FILM AND VIDEO

A Poet's Poet: The Legacy of Naomi Long Madgett, Writer and Director, Virgil Carr Center (Revised 2022)

Austere and Lonely Offices: Imaginings in the Poetry of Robert Hayden, Producer, Director and Writer (in production), 2015.

Reading Robert Hayden: Darwin T. Turner Discusses the Poetry of Robert Hayden, Director, 2014.

Star by Star: Naomi Long Madgett, Poet and Publisher, Co-Producer, penUltimate, Ltd. 2012.

The Black Unicorn: Dudley Randall and the Broadside Press. Director/Writer/Producer, 1996.

CHAPTERS WRITTEN

"The Unconquerable Josephine Baker: Raging War Against Fascism during World War II," in *Impressions of Paris*, Sylvie Blum, Ed. (forthcoming, 2023).

"People Who Have Done Bad Things: Police Detroit," in *Why We Can't Sing America*, Joyce Ann Joyce, Ed. (forthcoming, 2023)

"The Pan Damn It," *2020, The Year that Changed America*, Kevin Powell, editor. Amazon and Amazon Kindle, 2021.

"'Who's that Ni**a on that Nag': *Django Unchained* and the Return of the Blaxploitation Hero," *African American Cinema and Cultural Studies through Black Consciousness.* Mark A. Reid, ed. (Detroit: Wayne State University Press) 2020.

"James Baldwin and the Black Arts Movement," *James Baldwin in Context*. Quentin Miller, ed. (Cambridge, UK: University of Cambridge Press) 2020.

"From 1973 to Becoming 73, Jose-Angel Figueroa's Poetic Vision Spans Identities, Nations, and Literary Movements," in *Heartbeats, Rhythm and Fire* by Jose Figueroa, New York: Red Sugar Cane Press, 2019.

"Frances E. W. Harper: In the Situation of Ishmael," *Cambridge Companion to the Literature of the American Renaissance*. Christopher N. Phillips, ed. (Cambridge, UK: Cambridge University Press) 2019.

"The Police Was the Problem," *1967 Detroit Rebellion: Origins, Impacts and Legacies.* Joel Stone, ed. (Detroit: Wayne State University Press) 2017.

"A Rebellion is Not a Riot," *The Art of Rebellion*, Charles H. Wright Museum of African American History, 2018.

"Waiting for Smokey Robinson," *Heaven Was Detroit: Memories and Interpretations of Detroit Music, from Jazz to Hip Hop and Beyond*. Liebler, M.L., ed. Detroit, MI: Wayne State University Press, 2017.

"The Starlit Poetry of Naomi Long Madgett," *Naomi Long Madgett: 2012 Kresge Eminent Artist*. The Kresge Foundation, 2012.

"Disappearing Acts: Black Face and the Tyranny of Intellectual Imperialism," *Women of Color and Social Justice: Taking Their Rightful Place in Leadership*. Johnson III, Richard Gregory and Harris, G.L.A. eds. San Diego, CA: Birkdale Publishers, 2010.

"Trajectory of Inevitability: Remembering Michel Fabre," *A Gathering of Friends: Memoirs for Michel Fabre.* Fabre, Genevieve, ed. Paris, France: AFRAM Publications, 2010.

"The Poetics of Politics: The '68ers' and the Transcontinental Connections between Germans and African Americans." *Crossovers: African Americans and Germany*. Diedrich, Maria, Henrich, Jürgen. Green, Larry, eds. Frankfurt, Germany: Muenster, Germany: Verlag Publications, 2010.

"The Time of the Whirlwind and the Fire: Dudley Randall, the Heritage Series and the Broadside Press Connection," *The Heritage Series of Black Poetry, 1962–1975: A Research Compendium*. Bremen, Paul and Ramey, Lauri, eds. London, England: Ashgate Publishing, 2007.

"Poetry from Detroit's Black Bottom: The Tension between Belief and Ideology in the Words of Robert Hayden" in *Robert Hayden: Essays on the Poetry*. Chrisman, Robert and Goldstein, Larry, eds. Ann Arbor: University of Michigan Press, 2001.

"Afro-Centrics, Afro-Elitists, and Afro-Eccentrics: The Polarization of Black Studies Since the Student Struggles of the Sixties," *Dispatches from the Ebony Tower*. Marable, Manning, ed. New York: Columbia University Press, 2000.

"'Neath Sheltering Vines and Stately Palms" and "The Dialectics of Dialect Poetry." *Discarded Legacy, Poetry Criticism: Excerpts from Criticism of the Works of the Most Significant and Widely Studied Poets of the World*, Vol. 21, Gaffke, Carol T. and Sheets, Anna J. eds. Detroit & London: Gale Research, 1998.

"The Music in Afroamerican Poetry." *Sing the Sun Up: Creative Writing Ideas from African American Literature*, Thomas, Lorenzo, ed. New York: Teachers & Writers Collaborative, 1998.

"Frances E.W. Harper." *Encyclopedia of American Poetry*. Haralson. Eric, ed. Chicago and London: Fitzroy Publishers, 1998.

"Literacy and the Liberation of Bigger Thomas," *Approaches to Teaching Wright's Native Son*. Miller, James, ed. New York: Modern Language Association, Teaching World Literature Series, 1997.

Three essays on Frances E. W. Harper, "Two Offers," "Iola Leroy," "Sketches of Southern Life," in *The Oxford Companion to African American Literature*, edited by William Andrews, Frances Smith Foster and Trudier Harris. New York: Oxford University Press, 1996.

"Envisioning Freedom: Jazz, Film, Writing and the Reconstruction of American Thought," in *The Canon in the Classroom: The Pedagogical Implications of Canon Revision in American Literature,* edited by John Alberti. New York: Garland Publishing, 1995.

"Collard Greens, Clarence Thomas, and the High-Tech Rape of Anita Hill," in *Court of Appeals, e*dited by Robert Chrisman. New York: Ballantine Press, 1992

"The Salt in the Sugar: The Hot Reception of the Novel/Film, *The Color Purple*," in *Protest, Rebellion, and Dissent Within the Black Community,* edited by Berndt Ostendorf and Maria Diedrich. Tubingen. Germany: Gunter Narr Verlag Press, 1991.

"Cherokee Spirituality in Alice Walker's Meridian," *Minority Literatures of North America,* edited by Wolfgang Karrer. Tubingen, Germany: Gunter Narr Verlag Press, 1990.

"The Living Constitution: A Review," Wissenschaftliche Jahrestagung der Deutschen für Amerikastudien, Bremen (1987), *Gulliver: Deutsch-Englische Jahrbucher* 23, no 2, 1988.

"Song for Maya: A Discussion of the Poem by the Poet," *Missions in Conflict: U.S. - Mexican Relations and Chicano Culture.* Bardeleben, Bruce-Novoa, and Briesmeister, eds. Tubingen, Germany: Gunter Narr Verlag Press, 1986.

"Broadside Press 1975," *Broadside Memories*, edited by Dudley Randall. Detroit: Broadside Press, 1975.

Introduction, "Detroit City Poetry," *Abandon Automobile: Detroit City Poetry 2001*, Wayne State University Press, 2001. (Co-Authored)

EDITORSHIPS OF SERIES

Editorial Board, Wayne State University Press, 1995–22.

Editor, African American Life Series, Wayne State University Press, 1995–2022.

Contributing Editor, Made in Michigan Series, Wayne State University Press, 2010–22.

Contributing Editor, *The Black Scholar: Journal of Black Studies and Research*, 2013–20.

Editor. *Centennial Conference for Richard Wright*, American University of Paris, Special Issue for *The Black Scholar Journal*, 39, nos. 1 & 2, 2009.

Guest Editor. *The University of Michigan and the Anti-Affirmative Action Suits*. Special Issue, *The Black Scholar: Journal of Black Studies and Research* 32, no.1–2, Winter 2003.

Contributing Editor: *Drumvoices Revue* 2000, Special Millennium Issue, Southern Illinois University, 2000.

Assistant Editor, Broadside Press, Detroit, 1972–1977.

JOURNAL ARTICLES PUBLISHED

"Fred Was Feelin' It: Frederick Douglass, Gil Scott-Heron and Childish Gambino," www.Konch.org. Ishmael Reed., ed. (Spring, 2023).

"Requiem for Naomi Long Madgett," *The Langston Hughes Review*, Penn State University Press, Tony Bolden, Ed. (Spring, 2023).

"The Starlit Poetry of Naomi Long Madgett," The Poetry Foundation, www.Harriet.onlinejournal.com November 2021.

"The Coronavirus Diary," March 2020, Ishmael Reed, Editor, www.Konch.org.

"Double Consciousness and Double Entendre in *Get Out*," *Black Renaissance Noire Journal*, Quincy Troupe, ed., New York University, Institute for African American Affairs, NYU Press, Fall 2019.

"The Ghost Got It Wrong: Frances E. W. Harper and Toni Morrison, A Century A/Part," *Black Renaissance Noire Journal*, Quincy Troupe, ed., New York University, Institute for African American Affairs, NYU Press, Spring 2017.

"The Current State of Black Studies in the U.S.," Paradigm Shifts in Black Studies, Special Issue, Carsten Junker, ed. Zietschrift fur Anglistik und Amerikanistik*: Quarterly of Language, Literature and Culture*, Spring 2017.

"The Mystery of Romance in the Life and Poetics of Frances Ellen Watkins Harper, On the Recovery of Frances Ellen Watkins Harper's Forest Leaves": *Archives, Origins and African American Literature*, *Roundtable: The Journal of Early American Life*, Vol. 16, No. 2., Winter 2016.

"Richard Wright Centennial in Paris," *The Black Scholar: Journal of Black Studies and Research* 39: nos. 1 & 2, 2009.

"Red, White and the Blues: Translating Existentialism in Richard Wright's *Native Son* into Film," *The Black Scholar: Journal of Black Studies and Research* 39: nos. 1 & 2, 2009.

"Kenn Cox and Donald Walden: Free Jazz Radicals," "Working it Out," and "A Mingus Among Us, A Donald Walden Within Us, "*Against the Current* 139: no. 1, March/April 2009.

"Biographies, Autobiographies, and Memoirs, Taking Poetic License: a Poet Writing About Poets," *The Black Scholar* 38: nos. 2–3, 2008.

"Collateral Damage Sustained in the Film Crash," *Souls: A Critical Journal of Black Politics, Culture, and Society* 9, no. 3, 2007, The Institute for Research in African American Studies, Columbia University.

"Thomas Jefferson's Outside Squeeze," *Konch*. Reed, Ishmael, ed. Fall 2007. http://www.ishmaelreeedpub.com/, online journal.

"Disappearing Acts: Black Face and the Tyranny of the Academy: 1967–2005," *Konch*. Reed, Ishmael, ed. Winter 2006. http://www.ishmaelreeedpub.com/, online journal.

"The African American Presence and the Resolution of Race in *The Matrix Trilogy*, *Renaissance Noire* 5, No. 3, 2004, New York University, Department of Africana Studies.

"In Memoriam: Ronald Milner," *The Black Scholar: Journal of Black Studies and Research* 34, no. 4, 2004.

"A Horse of a Different Color." *The Black Scholar: Journal of Black Studies and Research*. 32, no. 1–2, 2004.

"'Roses and Revolutions,': Dudley Randall: Poet, Publisher, Critic and Champion of African American Literature Leaves a Legacy of Immeasurable Value," *The Black Scholar: Journal of Black Studies and Research* 31, no. 1, 2001.

"Remembering Dudley Randall," *Against the Current*, Vol. XV, No. 6, January-February, 2001.

"A Layover in Detroit, or Wherein Lies the Future of Black Studies," *Souls: A Critical Journal of Black Politics, Culture, and Society* 2, no. 3, 2000. The Institute for Research in African American Studies, Columbia University.

"*Prophets for a New Day*: The Cultural Activism of Gwendolyn Brooks, Margaret Danner, Margaret Burroughs and Margaret Walker During the Black Arts Movement," *Revista Caneria de Estudios Ingeles* 37, Universidad de la Laguna, Spain, 1998.

"Whose Jazz Is It Anyway?: Culture, Community and Survival," with Donald Walden. Publication of Conference Presentation: "April in Paris: African American Music and Europe" *Against the Current* 11, No. 6, 1997.

"Frances E. W. Harper's Legacy," *Against the Current* 10, no. 1, March-April 1995.

"Afro-Centrics, Afro-Elitists, and Afro-Eccentrics: The Polarization of Black Studies Since the Student Struggles of the Sixties," *Race & Reason* 1, no. 1, 1994, Columbia University.

"Canon Configuration for Ida B. Wells," *The Black Scholar: Journal of Black Studies and Research* 24: no. 1 & 2, 1994.

"Time Warp: A Historical Perspective on Two Novels by Frances E. W. Harper," *The Black Scholar: Journal of Black Studies and Research* 23: nos. 3 & 4, 1993.

"Holding a Torch for Black Americans," *The Black Scholar: Journal of Black Studies and Research* 23: no. 4, 1993.

"The Critical Mistreatment of Frances E.W. Harper," *Drumvoices: A Confluence of African American Art and Culture*, 2, no. 3 & 4, 1993.

"But Not the Blackness of Space: *The Brother From Another Planet*," *Journal of the Fantastic in Arts* 1, no. 3, 1989.

"Out of the Poetry Ghetto: The Life/Art Struggle of Small Black Publishers." *The Black Scholar: Journal of Black Studies and Research* 35, no.4, 1985.

INVITED REVIEW ARTICLES

"From the Ground Up to the Sky: The Artistic Gestures and Energy in the Works of Nicole MacDonald" with Maya Wynn Boyd, Review of art exhibit at the Detroit Contemporary Art Gallery, February 15, 2022.

"When the Script Sucks," The Battle of the Algiers Motel: A Critical Roundtable on Kathryn Bigelow's Detroit, *Cineaste*, Vol XLIII, No. 1, Winter 2017.

Review of *The Detroit Symphony Orchestra* (Wayne State University Press, 2016*)*, Michigan Radio, Broadcast, December 2016.

"Tearing Down Walls and Building Bridges: A Review of *Xicana Codex of Changing Consciousness Writings, 2000–2010* by Cherríe L. Moraga," *Criticism: Journal of Arts and Literature*, 2015. 57: 1.

Review of *Crusader for Justice: Federal Judge Damon J. Keith*, The *Michigan Chronicle*, October 15, 2014.

Review of *The Last Holiday* by Gil Scott-Heron, *Detroit Metro Times, August 11, 2012.*

"Icon from the Underground: The Brother From Another Planet." *City Arts Quarterly*, Detroit Council of the Arts 2: 3, 1987.

Review of The Oxford Anthology of African American Poetry, Rampersad, Arnold, ed. and Herbold, Hilary, associate ed. The *Black Scholar* 35. 5, 2006.

"Review of Thomas Sayers Ellis' *Genuine Negro Hero*." *African American Review*, Summer 13. 4, 2002.

Review of *Showing Our Colors: Afro-German Women Speak Out*, The *Black Scholar: Journal of Black Studies and Research* 22. 3, 1992.

Review of *Healing Heart* by Gloria G. Hull. *The Black Scholar: Journal of Black Studies and Research*, 18. 2, 1989.

Review of Jayne Cortez's *Coagulations*. *The Black Scholar: Journal of Black Studies and Research* 14. 3, 1985.

Review of June Jordan's *Living Room*. *The Black Scholar: Journal of Black Studies and Research* 14. 2, 1985.

"The Whitman Awakening in June Jordan's Poetry: Passion." *Obsidian* 7. 2 & 3, 1981.

Review of *I Love Myself When I Am Laughing... A Zora Neale Hurston Reader*. *The Black Scholar: Journal of Black Studies and Research*, 9. 4, 1980.

Review of *Exits and Entrances* By Naomi Madgett, *The Black Scholar: Journal of Black Studies and Research* 8. 3, 1979.

Review of *Black Rituals* by Sterling Plumpp. *Black Books Bulletin* 1. 4, 1973.

"The Elements of Blindness in Chester Himes' *Hot Day Hot Night*," *Black World*, Hoyt Fuller, Ed. March 1972.

EDITORIAL

Freelance writer, *Detroit Metro Times*, 1980–82.

Freelance writer, *Detroit Sun*, 1975–76.

Kresge Arts in Detroit

Our Congratulations

Influential. Distinguished. Renowned.

Expansive as they are, these words do not capture the prolific literary achievements, cultural contributions, and artistic impact of 2023 Kresge Eminent Artist Dr. Melba Joyce Boyd.

Dr. Boyd is a native Detroiter, poet, scholar, editor, essayist and filmmaker. Her prose honors local and global icons, chronicles historic events, explores the lives and experiences of Black Detroiters, and calls clearly for justice and accountability that are long overdue.

She is the award-winning author with 13 books to her name plus over 100 published essays; her work has appeared in anthologies, academic journals, cultural periodicals, and newspapers in the United States and Europe.

Dr. Boyd's life and work are intertwined with the history of Detroit and its legacy of groundbreaking, game-changing artists. She was assistant editor to Dudley Randall, (who founded Broadside Press) and refers to Randall and Naomi Long Madgett — 2012 Kresge Eminent Artist, founder of Lotus Press, and like Randall, a Detroit Poet Laureate — as her "literary parents."

Many of Dr. Boyd's works open with piercing cadence and content that set the table for the story she has prepared for readers and listeners to receive. Her pointed poetry is an amalgamation of history and art, a mingling of fact and feeling — and the space where the two are indistinguishable.

It is an honor to celebrate Dr. Melba Joyce Boyd's lifetime of achievements — and add the 15th Kresge Eminent Artist Award to an extensive list of well-deserved awards and accolades.

Christina deRoos
Director, Kresge Arts in Detroit

Kresge Arts in Detroit Advisory Panel, 2022–2023

Dr. Melba Joyce Boyd was named the 2023 Kresge Eminent Artist by a distinguished peer group of metro Detroit artists and arts professionals:

Gil Ashby
Artist;
Associate Professor,
Illustration Chair (2000–10),
College for Creative Studies;
2011 NY Society of Illustration
Distinguished Educator

Kahn Santori Davison
Writer/Photographer,
Detroit Metro Times and
Model D Media;
2015 Kresge Artist Fellow

Wendell Harrison
Artistic Director, Rebirth Inc.;
Member/Awardee,
Chamber Music America;
2018 Kresge Eminent Artist

Scheherazade Washington Parrish
Interdisciplinary Artist;
Co-Director, Detroit Lit

Grace Serra
Art Curator, Wayne State University
and University of Michigan

The Eminent Artist Award

Since 2008 the Kresge Eminent Artist Award has been presented annually to honor one exceptional literary, visual, film or performing artist whose influential body of work, lifelong professional achievements and proven, continued commitment to the Detroit cultural community are evident.

The Kresge Eminent Artist Award celebrates artistic innovation and rewards integrity and depth of vision with the financial support of $50,000. The Kresge Eminent Artist Award is unrestricted and is given annually to an artist who has lived and worked in Wayne, Oakland or Macomb counties for a significant number of years. The annual Kresge Eminent Artist Award, Kresge Artist Fellowships and Gilda Awards – administered by the Kresge Arts in Detroit office of the College for Creative Studies – reflect The Kresge Foundation's belief that supports for artists themselves are integral to a robust arts and culture ecosystem across metropolitan Detroit.

Kresge Eminent Artists 2008–2022

2022
Olayami Dabls

2019
Gloria House

2021
Shirley Woodson

2018
Wendell Harrison

2020
Marie Woo

2017
Patricia Terry-Ross

2016
Leni Sinclair

2012
Naomi Long Madgett

2015
Ruth Adler Schnee

2011
Bill Harris

2014
Bill Rauhauser

2009
Marcus Belgrave

2013
David DiChiera

2008
Charles McGee

Credits and Acknowledgements

About The Kresge Foundation

The Kresge Foundation was founded in 1924 to promote human progress. Today, Kresge fulfills that mission by building and strengthening pathways to opportunity for low-income people in America's cities, seeking to dismantle structural and systemic barriers to equality and justice. Using a full array of grant, loan and other investment tools, Kresge invests more than $160 million annually to foster economic and social change.

Board of Trustees

Cecilia Muñoz,
Board Chair

James L. Bildner
Richard Buery Jr.
Kathy Ko Chin
Audrey Choi
John Fry
Saunteel Jenkins
Cynthia Kresge*
Scott Kresge **
Maria Otero
Paula B. Pretlow
Suzanne Shank
Rip Rapson, President
and CEO (ex-officio)

*retired June 2023
**joined June 2023

Publication Team

Jennifer Kulczycki
Director, External Affairs
and Communications

Julie A. Bagley
Communications Assistant,
External Affairs
and Communications

W. Kim Heron
Senior Communications Officer,
External Affairs
and Communications

Alejandro Herrera
Senior Graphic Designer,
External Affairs
and Communications

Creative Team

Nichole M. Christian
Creative Director,
Editor & Lead Writer

Ed Ryan (E-A-R)
Art Director & Designer

Complimentary copies of this monograph and others in the Kresge Eminent Artist series are available while supplies last. All monographs are also available for free download by visiting kresge.org/eminentartist.

Unless otherwise noted, photos used throughout this monograph are from the personal collection of Dr. Melba Joyce Boyd. Every effort has been made to locate and credit the holders of copyrighted materials.

Acknowledgements

The creative team extends its sincerest gratitude to Dr. Melba Joyce Boyd for opening the doors of her home and the pages of an inspiring life.

Our deepest gratitude also goes out to photographer Erin Kirkland, audio producer Zak Rosen and artist Maya Boyd for their creative and thoughtful contributions to *The Book of Melba.* Sincere thanks also to Melba's sister Dorothy Donise Davis for generously sharing family photos.

Index

This index is sorted letter-by-letter. Italic page locators indicate photographs on the page.

A

Abandon Automobile: Detroit City Poetry 2001 (poetry collection), 23, 98

B

Baldwin, James, 66, *67*
"The Bass Is Woman" (poem), 88
Belgrave, Marcus, 87, *115*
Bethune, Mark, 34, 39, 99–100
Black Arts Movement, 68, 69–70, 97
Black World (periodical), *69*
"Blow Marcus Blow" (poem), 87
blues music sky of mourning, the German poems (poetry collection), *19*, 21
"B Movie" (poem; Scott-Heron), 102
Boyd, Bernice, 50
Boyd, Dorothy. *See* Clore, Dorothy
Boyd, John Percy, Jr., 34–35, *35,* 37, 38, 39, 42, 49, 56, *57,* 99–100
Boyd, John Percy, Sr., *48,* 49–50, 54, 56
Boyd, John Percy, III, *20,* 21, 50, *58*
Boyd, Maya Wynn, 21, 26, *32*
    art by, *29*
    on Melba, 32–33
Boyd, Melba Joyce
    artistic portrayals, *29, 73*
    artist statement, 12–13
    awards, 11, 19, 26, 32, 104, 106–107, 112
    bibliography, 103, 107–110
    biography and family, 1, 14, 15, 16, *20,* 21, 26, 32, 34–35, 38, 42–43, *46, 47,* 49–59, *51, 52, 54, 55,* 63, 99–100
    career, 14–16, 18–27, 35, 40, 41–42, 68–72, 96, 105–106, 112
    as community cultural influence, 11, 15, 18, 23, 24–25, 26–27, 28–43, 83, 112
    creative/work processes, 13, 22–23, 82
    education, 18, 54, *62, 63, 64,* 65–69, 97–98, 100–101, 105
    essays and articles, 96–102, 103, 108–110
    literary influences, 65, 66–69, 100–101
    peers and community on, 11, 14–27, 31–43
    photographs of, *9, 10, 12, 15, 17, 20, 25, 32,* 44, *46, 51, 52, 54, 57, 58, 60, 63, 74, 76, 77, 104, 111*
    poetry, 13, 16, 18, 19, 21, 22–23, 25, 26, 31, 32–33, 35, 37, 38, 78–95, 98, 100–101, 103, 107–108, 112
    work content and themes, 22–23, 24–25, 98
Boyd, Richard, 53
Boyd, Sandra, 38, 55, *57, 58*
Broadside Press
    Black Arts Movement, 69–70, 97
    Randall's and Boyd's work, 18, 19, 32, *33,* 35, 37, 69–71, 98, 103
Brown, Hayward, 34, 39, 99–100
Brown, Peter and Odessa, 50
Brown, Semaj, 38, 40
"burial of a building" (poem), 25, 84–85

C

"C'est une Histoire Extraordinaire" (poem), 92–93
Chicago, Illinois, 97
Christian, Nichole M., 14–27, 28–43
Civil Rights Movement, 65, 66, 68, 70–72, 97, 100–101
Clore, Dorothy, *47,* 54, *55,* 63
Clore, John, 63
Clore, Siegel, II, 56, *59,* 63
Clore (Davis), Dorothy, *57*
Comer, Nandi, *74*
Cooper, Anna Julia, 42
creative process, 13, 22–23, 82

D

Davis, Dorothy Donise, *58*
Death Dance of a Butterfly (poetry collection), *33,* 106
"death of a time" (poem), 90–91
deRoos, Christina, 112
Detroit, Michigan
    Boyd history, 34–38, 40–41, *46–48,* 49–50, 56, *62,* 63, 65, 99–100
    Boyd's cultural influence, 11, 15, 18, 23, 24–25, 26–27, 28–43, 83, 112
    history, 25, 34–38, *39,* 40–41, 49, 50, 63, 72, 97
    maps, *62*
    poetry of and about, 18, 23, 25, 32–33, 38, 40, 41, 65, 69–70, *73,* 80–81, 83, 84–85, 87, 97, 98
    public art, *73*
Discarded Legacy: Politics and Poetics in the Life of Frances E. W. Harper, 1825–1911 (Boyd), 26, *33,* 100

E

Ebony (periodical), 68

F

Falconer, Nancy, 24, *58*
"false moonscrape umbrellas, for George Tysh" (poem), 23
Ferrell, Charles, 31
Fosten, Inez Boyd, 53
Franklin, Aretha, *30,* 31
Fuller, Hoyt W., 68, *69,* 70

G

Germany: travel, teaching, and writings, 18, *19,* 21, 72, 101–102

H

Harper, Frances E. W., 26, 33, 54, *61,* 72, 100
Hayden, Marion, 24, *25,* 88
Hayden, Robert, 41, 65
Hill, Anita, 99
Himes, Chester, 68, *69*

I

international travel, work, and publishing, 18, *20,* 21, 26, 72, 101–102
"in the absence of meaning" (poem), 22
"Intro: the fourteenth flamingo" (poem), 101

K

Kenyon, James, 16, *20*
King, Martin Luther, Jr., 65, 68, 100–101
Kresge Foundation Eminent Artist Award, 11, 26, 113
    Boyd (2023), 11, 26, 32, 104, 112
        previous recipients, 11, 18, 27, 87, 114–115

L

Letters to Ché (poetry collection), 22, *23*
Liebler, M.L., 23
Luvall, Alex, 63, 65
Luvall, Rosemarie, 65, 89

M

Macdonald, Nicole, *73*
Madgett, Naomi Long, 18, 70, *73,* 98, *115*
"A Mingus Among Us and a Walden Within Us" (poem), 86
Moore, Opal, 41–42
murals, *73*

N

NAACP Image Award, 19, 32, 106
Nichols, John, 38, *39*
"1965" (poem), 79, 98
Nurullah, Shahida, *25*

P

Parrish, Scheherazade Washington, 26
Pershing High School, *62, 63,* 65, 101
police oppression and violence, 34–38, *39,* 40–41, 99–100
Pouncy, Sonya, 33
the province of literary cats (poetry collection), 23, 25

R

Randall, Dudley
    art and photographs, 71, 73
    biographies, 18, 19, 97–98
    Broadside Press, 18, 19, 33, 35, 69–71
    relationship, influence, and mentoring, 33, 41, 65, 69, 70–71, 97–98
    students of, 68
Rapson, Rip, 10–11
Rashid, Frank, 40–41
Reagan, Ronald, 101, 102
Reed, Gregory J., 18
"Rock Steady for the Queen of Soul" (poem), 31
"the rose in the garden" (poem), 49, 89
Rosen, Zak, 45
Roses and Revolutions: The Selected Writings of Dudley Randall (Boyd), 18, 19, 32, 106
Ryder, Mitch, 101

S

Scott-Heron, Gil, 101–102
Second Great Migration, 49–50
Serra, Grace, 26
sexual assault, 98–99
Smith, Percy, *54*
"somebody stole your tennis shoes" (poem), 95
Sound Stories (audio files), 44–45, 54, 58, 66, 70, 72
Stop the Robberies, Enjoy Safe Streets (STRESS; Detroit Police Dept.), 34–35, 38, *39,* 40–41, 100–101

T

Taylor, Bernice, 53
Taylor, Great Grandmother, *55*
Teichman, Dennis, 16
"this museum was once a dream" (poem), 25, 83
Thomas, Clarence, 99
"To Darnell and Johnny" (poem), 35, 37
Troupe, Quincy, 35, 40
"2001" (poem), 94

U

University of Iowa, 41–42

V

"the view of blue" (poem), 25

W

Walden, Donald, 86
Walker, Alice, 35
Ware, Sandra, 42–43
Wayne State University, 21, *25,* 26–27, 38, 42, 66, *73,* 105
"We Almost Lost Detroit" (song; Scott-Heron), 102
Western Michigan University, *64,* 65, 68, 69, 97–98, 100, 105
"we want our city back" (poem), 25, 80–81
Winfield, Owen Darnell, 34–35, *35,* 37, 38, 56
"wingless spiders, Bremen, December 17, 1983" (poem), 21, 101
Wrestling with the Muse: Dudley Randall and the Broadside Press (Boyd), 18, 19, 32, *33,* 34, 38, 70, *71,* 97–98, 106
Wynn, Owen, *52,* 53
Wynn, Sarah, *52,* 53, *55*

Y

"yari yari: writing for the future" (poem), 13, 82
Young, Coleman A., 38

The Book of Melba
©2023 The Kresge Foundation
All rights reserved
Printed in the United States
of America

First edition
ISBN: 978-1-7328601-4-8

Requests for additional copies of
this book, or permission to reprint or
reproduce any portion of this work,
should be submitted to:

The Kresge Foundation
3215 W. Big Beaver Rd.
Troy, Michigan 48084
media@kresge.org

Printing
University Lithoprinters
Ann Arbor, MI

Design
E-A-R

Typefaces
ABC ROM Family
by Dinamo (CH)